The Uses of Culture
Education and the Limits of Ethnic Affiliation

Cameron McCarthy

Routledge
New York   London

Published in 1998 by
Routledge
29 West 35th Street
New York, NY 10001

Published in Great Britain in 1998 by
Routledge
11 New Fetter Lane
London EC4P 4EE

Printed in the United States of America on acid-free paper
Design: Jack Donner

Library of Congress Cataloging-in-Publication Data

McCarthy, Cameron.
The uses of culture: education and the limits of ethnic affiliation / Cameron
  McCarthy.
    p.   cm.
Includes bibliographical references and index.
ISBN 0–415–91299–7 — ISBN 0–415–91300–4 (pbk.)
1. Educational sociology. 2. Culture. 3. Ethnicity. 4. Race awareness.
5. Multicultural education. 6. Popular culture. I. Title. II. Series.
LC191.2.M33   1997
306.43—dc21   97–19763
                                                                  CIP

For Angharad

CONTENTS

ACKNOWLEDGMENTS

The task of writing *The Uses of Culture,* though always intensely personal and intensely "private," has throughout benefited from its mediation by collective support. Many of my friends willed me forward with this book from its gestation. Michael Apple, my academic mentor and editor, suggested a book summing up my work on race and identity to date. The book not only tries to do this, but also it reflects my doubts and uncertainties about current theorizing on race, identity, and representation. I am particularly grateful to Michael for his encouragement with respect to a manuscript over which I have labored and struggled more than I have in previous work.

I owe special thanks to my students and colleagues in the departments of Curriculum and Instruction and Educational Policy Studies, and in the Institute of Communication Research at the University of Illinois. Particular acknowledgment must be made of the critical attention to my work that the Cultural Understanding Reading and Research Collaborative of students and faculty at the University of Illinois gave to my manuscript. Members of the Collaborative—Ed Buendia, Stephen David, Greg Dimitriadis, Nadine Dolby, Grace Giorgio, Abebe Fisseha, Heriberto Godina, Rochelle Gutierrez, Maureen Hogan, Lenora de la Luna, Shuaib Meecham, Carol Mills, Susan Noffke, Swarna Rajagopalan, Alicia Rodriguez, Maria Seferian, Teresa Souchet, K. E. Supryia, and Carrie Wilson-Brown—must be thanked individually and collectively for their many helpful suggestions.

A generous grant from the Campus Research Board of the University of Illinois provided me with the very competent and enthusiastic research assistance of Paula Saukko and Sylvia Allegretto. I am eternally grateful for the criticisms and editorial suggestions that Paula and Sylvia offered to me. These two provoked me to rethink significant aspects of *The Uses of Culture* at a point when I thought I was ready to put the manuscript away.

A special thanks is due to Professor Clifford Christians, Chair of the Institute of Communication Research at the University of Illinois, for his encouragement and advice. I am also enormously grateful to

Lawrence Grossberg, who carefully read many of the essays included in this volume at a very early stage.

Throughout the torture of writing *The Uses of Culture*, my keenest critic and supporter has been my companion, Angharad Valdivia. I believe this book would not have been written this way without her presence and gentle but trenchant insight.

PREFACE

Epic discourse is a discourse handed down by tradition. By its very nature the epic of the absolute past is inaccessible to personal experience and does not permit an individual, personal point of view or evaluation. One cannot glimpse it, grope for it, take it apart, penetrate into its core. It is given solely as tradition, sacred and sacrosanct, evaluated in the same way by all and demanding a pious attitude to itself.
—Mikhail Bakhtin, *The Dialogic Imagination*, 1981, p. 16

We are living in a time of an extraordinary ethnicization of culture. Much of this cultural balkanization is translated through processes of what I wish to call alienated representation of the other; that is, practices of defining one's identity through the negation of the other—practices that Friedreich Nietzsche (1967) called "ressentiment." A keenly contested site has been enjoined in schooling as socially embattled majority and minority groups compete with each other in the public sphere and in the domain of culture—the domain of signs. The world, all of a sudden, has become a very crowded place, and communities of minorities and postcolonial immigrants now populate metropolitan schools and suburban towns to an extent and in a manner that deeply unsettles racially hegemonic groups.

In educational life, these matters have taken on a particularly racially inflamed tone at late-century. The publication in the late eighties and early nineties of culturally narrow-minded texts such as Alan Bloom's *The Closing of the American Mind* (1987), Dinesh D'Souza's *Illiberal Education* (1991), and Roger Kimball's *Tenured Radicals* (1990) and the neo-nationalist response of some minority school critics ushered in a new phase of eruptive particularism in educational discourses on culture and school knowledge. This new phase in educational and social life is marked by a revivified investment in ethnic symbolism and an almost epic revalorization of the ethnic histories and origins of some embattled dominant and subordinate groups. We are living in a time in which

racial hysteria and racial anxiety ride the undersides of the public discourse on schooling and society as rapid demographic changes alter the
racial and ethnic landscape of America. These developments have
spawned what I wish to call the new essentialisms that have infected educational discourses on knowledge and culture. An increasingly rigid
and constricted language has overtaken the discussion of curriculum
reform in the Age of Difference. This is poignantly reflected in contemporary discourses of biological and cultural exceptionalism generated
by books such as Richard Herrnstein and Charles Murray's *The Bell
Curve* (1994) and William Bennett's *The Book of Virtues* (1994), and by
Leonard Jeffries' glib pronouncements (Dyson, 1993).

The Uses of Culture is written against the backdrop of racial anxiety in
the educational field. I write with the unique sense of double vision, the
double perspective of a child of both domination and privilege—a postcolonial subject displaced to the first world. Throughout the nine essays
published in this book I aim at an intervention in the increasingly constricted and narrow-minded field of racial politics in education. The
essays take as a central problem the limitations of the cultural excep-
tionalisms that underwrite racial identity politics in the educational field
and in the broader popular culture. More significantly, the book takes a
detour through autobiography, popular culture, and the literature of
postcolonial societies as strategic sites for understanding the trials and
tribulations of the races in the first world. In addition, I attempt,
through a critical revision of the multicultural thesis, to formulate a
notion of education as the preparation for global reality. In all these matters race is never an absolute structuring force, but is instead one variable in an immensely rich and complex human environment. The
struggle is always to understand racial dynamics in the light of other dynamic variables such as class, gender, nation, and sexual orientation. The
intellectual project that I undertake here is to re-narrate the story of
racial affiliation and racial antagonism from a plurality of vantage points
inside and outside official culture and education and within the literature and popular culture of mass society in the metropole and the periphery alike. The nine essays included in this volume are not a linear
statement, but rather nine different meditations on the topics of culture,
race, identity, and multiculturalism written at a time when these issues
require urgent intellectual and programmatic attention.

ENGLISH RUSTICS
IN BLACK SKIN
Cultural Hybridity and Racial
Identity at the End of the Century

> Take him and cut him out in little stars,
> And he will make the face of heav'n so fine
> That all the world will be in love with Night
> And pay no worship to the garish sun. . .
> —Shakespeare, *Romeo and Juliet*, Act II, Sc.ii

> The mind of man is capable of anything—because everything is in
> it, all the past as well as all the future.
> —Conrad, *Heart of Darkness and Other Tales*, 1992, p. 186

> Ah! The whole diaspora shakes in my skin.
> —Anthony Kellman, *"Isle Man,"* 1993, p. 15

Within the past few years, I have come to the growing recognition that my writing about race and identity has been a form of postcolonial therapy, an exercise in opening up and pasting over contradictions of knowledge, place, context, and belonging. Writing for me, as I imagine it is for all intellectuals pursuing these topics, is as much a tortuous act of concealment and reinscription as it is one of transcending disclosure. Consider the vast sea of sociological ink now being spilled on the topics of class, race, and identity. Consider the boatloads of paper afloat on these subjects. Can we really argue that this ever-expanding volume of writing has led us to other than a very partial, adumbrated understanding of the opera-

tion of these dynamics? Can any of us really claim that we have come to a final or definitive understanding of racial logics or the operation of identity formation?

Here, at the end of the twentieth century—the great information age, the age of hypermodernization that classical social scientists and their disciples had told us would usher in the withering away of encrusted and sedimented atavism—we are faced in human societies with the unleashing of ever more virulent forms of particularism and localism operating in politics and popular culture. As a disturbing instance, nationalism and xenophobia in Europe—in the former Yugoslavia, in Germany and France—rip at the heart of the great icons of civilization in the West; a civilization against which everything in the third world and everything within the underclasses of the metropole are counterposed. On the continents of Africa, Asia, and Latin America, the politics of identity has been fought out in bloody skirmishes and long nights of horror such as those of Rwanda and Somalia, and the excesses of protofascist regimes in Indonesia and in Guatemala—just to mention a few examples of spectacularly gruesome forms of racial/ethnic cruelty.

As an academic who has over the last decade sometimes pontificated on matters of race and identity, I must admit a sense of bewilderment at the endless stream of racial cruelty that resides in the hearts of human beings in our relations with each other across the globe. Contemplating race relations in this country, I am both enraged and dismayed by the virulence of the hostilities and resentments unleashed in America against its disenfranchised Latino/a and African American inner-city poor. At the same time, I am revolted by suburban excesses and the salivatory prosecution of suburban will in the politics of both liberal and conservative politicians and policy intellectuals. In these matters, the contemporary observer on race and identity simply walks in the footsteps laid down in the sands of time. It was, after all, the great colonial novelist Joseph Conrad who, in Heart of Darkness, *proffered his own disorientation on identity questions through the narrating persona of Marlow. Reflecting on the exorbitant atrocities perpetrated by imperialism in Africa, Marlow uses a nostrum to effectively distance himself from Europe's project of subjugation of the native: "The mind of man is capable of anything—because everything is in it, all the past as well as all the future" (p. 186). As a writer, Conrad, too, was implicated. He was a product of Europe, a seafarer, whose characters, like himself, pursued their imperial fantasies and desires onto the bodies of the native even as they tormented themselves about the "evil in the hearts of men." Like Conrad, every writer has his demons. And, "Like a jig shakes the loom/Like a web is spun the pattern/All of us are involved/All of us are consumed" (Carter, 1979, p. 44). Is it the demons in our hearts that we write to exorcise? As it was with Conrad's fiction, is, perhaps, the ultimate purpose of our writing the great disavowal of our own implication in life's history? In racial matters, is the postcolonial intellectual, indeed, washed in the blood of the lamb?*

Perhaps every postcolonial writer is a descendant of the forces that produced Conrad's phosphorescent naturalism, Conrad's blindspots and his all-consuming evasion of the role of the bourgeois self in the trauma of the native. On this matter "truth will not out." In the bright gleam of the realist fiction of the novelist, the anthropologist, the social scientist, the historian, and the educator hides the entrails of the imperialist lie. The author's claim to the vantage point beyond passion, beyond complicity and collusion, is not to be trusted. The author writing on race and identity conceals as much as he discloses. The intellectual observer, it would turn out, would have his stake in the apprehension and containment of the native. He, too, would have his own dreaming map of possession and rambunctious ownership. As Wilson Harris (1960) suggests in The Palace of the Peacock, *"Donne, too, was my brother" (p. 42). The colonizer would inhabit the body of the colonized. The colonial text would freeze and fix the native in the stillness of eternity. The colonizing text of the anthropologist ethnographer would close and bind the frame of the village. The urban sociologist would tell it like it is about underclass fecundity and degeneracy. For years and years, the student of history, anthropology, sociology, and education would read and perform these texts of ethnicity, of the self, and other. And then one day, the bright, motivated student, too, would arrive at the place of her/his calling, would become an anthropologist, a sociologist, and a writer of fictions about others. The intellectual had finally reproduced himself. The newborn academic, the living Narcissus, would deploy his gaze on the world with the fervor of a brand new Baby Bell.*

The postcolonial intellectual, the child of the Native and the King, always disavowed his own participation in this hypocrisy of completeness and the hierarchy of the global racial order. He, too, maintained his innocence. Dressed in the hand-me-downs of Prospero, he declared his blamelessness before the world and before his peers in the American academy. But truth be told, in the matter of racial identity formation, the postcolonial intellectual also is a creature of paradox: he has, for instance, an enormous appetite for the imperial symbolic, fine garments, literature, and haute cuisine while ceaselessly denouncing imperialism's excesses at home and abroad. I am a child of that paradox: the product of the exorbitant British presence in the Caribbean and the African slave who would be put out into the fields to work, and chained and bridled at the door. I am, too, part of that peculiar progeny of British imperialism whom Sidney Greenfield (1968) would call "English rustics in black skin."

The Uses of Culture *is written from this perspective of radical instability with respect to race-based forms of knowing and identification. It is written from the point of view of the perishability of the sociological understanding of the race question. It is written to seek out racial knowledge in places other than that of controlled study or the omniscient intent to organize the field of race relations theory, or the ethnographic excursion into the colonized life world of the other. It seeks out new understandings in new places: in the realms of popular culture, in the realms of literature, in the realms of imagination, in the realms of the filmic fantasy, and in the quiet agonism of postcolonial self-exploration and self-understanding. I speak for all those lost souls, who, like Derek Walcott, are "divided to the vein," and who—may God grant us the courage—find solace only in the exploration (1986, p. 18). This is the enigma of arrival of the postcolonial intellectual. In the matter of her/his investigation of the subject of conflicted racial identity formation, the postcolonial soul can know no peace.*

USES OF CULTURE

I begin this book, then, with a confession: all along, my writing on race in the United States has been informed by an attempt to straddle, to frantically stabilize, the conflicted biography of being born and educated in the periphery, Barbados, and coming into academic practice as an immigrant intellectual operating in the imperial center—the United States. My understanding of race, my foregrounding of its instabilities, its "nonsynchrony," as I called it in earlier work (McCarthy, 1988), is more than a little propelled by my own autobiographical elopement or displacement from the third world to the imperial center, home of "the great Satan."

I live everyday, like Ishmael in Herman Melville's *Moby Dick* (1851), in danger of being swallowed up and consumed in the churning belly of the Whale. I proceed with the deepest sense that there is a complexity to the story of race that writing merely adumbrates and never fully discloses. This is the paradox of all postcolonial intellectual writing on the varied forms of life and the differentiated cultural and economic realities of the metropole and the periphery alike. While I will not continue this essay in the confessional mode, it must be understood that everything that follows herein is in fact informed by the postcolonial predicament: the reality of perhaps permanent exile or banishment from any singular or fixed community and the attendant loss of full understanding of one's racial self. The imperial inheritance is finally a bag of gold, a bag of bones (Morrison, 1977).

THE ENGLISH BOOK

> *There is a scene in the cultural writings of English colonialism which repeats so insistently after the early nineteenth century—and, through that repetition, so triumphantly* inaugurates *a literature of empire—that I am bound to repeat it once more. It is the scenario, played out in the wild and wordless wastes of colonial India, Africa, the Caribbean, of the sudden, fortuitous discovery of the English book.*
> —Bhabha, *The Location of Culture*, 1994, p. 102

One of the limitations in current postcolonial theory and methodology regarding the analysis of racial identity and center-periphery relations— and indeed this is true of other critical minority discourses such as Afrocentrism and multiculturalism—is the failure of proponents to account for the conditions of production of their own intellectual work and their contradictory interests and affiliations. As Ali Behdad (1993) has pointed out, postcolonial theorists often present the analysis of center periphery relations within a zero-sum framework in which all agency, power, and moral responsibility emanate and flow from the center. The postcolonial theorist therefore appoints her/himself as a stand-in or proxy for the oppressed third world; a third world of the imaginary—a world that is unstratified, and uniformly underdeveloped—one in which the social field has been completely leveled by the mechanisms of exploitation and cultural domination.

Even more critically, in the work of some writers such as Molefi Asante (1993), Martin Carnoy (1974), Philip Altbach (1987), and Michael Parenti (1993), the imperial text, the text of colonial education, and Euroamerican canonical literature, tends to deliver reproductive (neo)colonial effects, seemingly untouched by indigenous practices or movements. Within these frameworks, the dwellers of postcolonial societies are, too often, hypothetical subjects, model addressees of colonizing discourses. Absent are the voices, cultural practices, and meaning of style of concrete, historical postcolonial and indigenous minority subjects. Even more disturbing is the methodological tendency to abrogate the whole field of accommodations, negotiations, and trestles of association and affiliation that link dominant and dominated political and cultural entities both locally and globally.

In *The Uses of Culture*, I take a different view of the dynamics of culture and race. I point to interconnections and continuities between prima facie racially and ethnically antagonistic groups (for example, the continuities of theme and form between Anglo-colonial novelists like Joseph Conrad and Afro-diasporic and anti-colonial writers such as Chinua Achebe or George Lamming). I also call attention to the contradictions within atavistically declared "pure" racial or ethnic communities (for instance, radical class tensions within the black communities of South Africa or the United States and the class hierarchies within the third world). One never fully knows with terms such as "race," "identity," or "culture." To study race, identity, or culture, and to intervene in their fields of effects, one must be prepared to live with extraordinary complexity and variability of meaning.

The texts and performativity of these constructs are always subject to aberrant decodings, aberrant meanings, and the dynamic play of histories and contexts. Permit me to relate three brief vignettes that illustrate the dynamic encounter between racially dominant and subaltern cultural forms in which processes of rearticulation constantly subvert the putative stability of center-periphery relations. The first story is autobiographical, foregrounding my encounter with hegemonic English and American literature as an undergraduate student at the Cave Hill campus of the University of the West Indies in Barbados in the late '70s; the second story highlights an example of the unexpected association between canonical literature and the rise of radical vernacular poetry in the Caribbean; and the third story is one told by Manthia Diawara of the subversive impact of African-American popular music in the '60s on French Africa and the way it functioned as an alternative cultural capital. These three stories illustrate the instability of racial meanings and challenge any narrow-minded construct of culture as ethnocentric property. They also foreground the radical, multiple effects that cultural forms release in everyday human encounters across the divides of nation, locality, and race.

STORY I: ANGLO-AMERICAN CULTURE WAR

One of the contradictions of cultural production in the third world, even in the postcolonial era, is the multiplicity of surreptitious, and not so surreptitious, lines of connection that link the postcolony to the metropole. The postcolony is not ever simply an original entity unto itself, shorn of the imprint and trace of the metropole. It is in many ways an impure copy full of the warp and woof of empire—an alloy of many racial, cultural, and economic metals, so to speak. Formal and informal cultural life in education and society reveal these connections in the everyday existence of the postcolonial subject. I can speak of these matters of cultural hybridity firsthand. Growing up as a child in Barbados in the '60s and '70s, one existed in a constant state of negotiation between the cultural form of England and that of the emergent post-independence island. Education was a particularly poignant site of the transaction of the competing needs, desires, and interests of the metropole and the indigene. Curriculum content, school ritual, and the formal history of the school system pointed to England. Every single important examination was either set or marked in the metropole. For instance, my high school "advanced level" examinations were the matriculation exams for Cambridge University. Examinations in Barbados were truly external and "objective"—we were the subject-objects of British cultural suzerainty.

As a youth, my social fate was in the hands of the markers of the General Certificate of Education of the Cambridge Examination Board. Passes or failures in these exams, which one sat at the end of high school, had material social meaning in Barbados. This arrangement continued into university, where again the University of the West Indies followed a practice of requiring all end-of-year examinations to be vetted by outside examiners mainly from England, but occasionally from the United States and elsewhere.

Often, these outside "monitors," as they were called, demonstrated their eminence by giving lectures to students when they were visiting. On one such occasion, the outside examiner for my American fiction course came to give a lecture on Ernest Hemingway's novels. Here was one of the incredibly ironic, but normally unremarked, moments of the postcolonial situation in Barbados: an American authority on a "great" American fiction writer giving a presentation to the Caribbean students of an American fiction class normally taught by an "eminent" Englishman. There we were, caught in the crossfire of the postpartum Anglo-American war over culture. In the University of the West Indies' Program in English Studies, all the American authors, ancient or modern, black or white, were stuck in the American literature course and separated out from the course called "The Moderns." The latter course of study was reserved for the great British writers, which included one luminous American transplant to England: T. S. Eliot. The "eminent American scholar" gave his lecture on the greatness of Hemingway's fiction. The Barbadian students didn't buy it and pointed out the technical flaws of Hemingway's novels insistently. The eminent American scholar floundered on questions that focused on the flawed love scene between Jordan and Maria in *For Whom the Bell Tolls* in which the narrator utters those incredible words: "And the earth moved from under her feet." The eminent American scholar was a bit flustered, the eminent English scholar looked gleeful. A great victory was won that day for Great Britain by the educated troops of "Little England." Remarkably, I got a call a few days after this Anglo-American skirmish from the gleeful English lecturer congratulating me for my critical challenges to the "orthodoxy" of the American: "He" did not appreciate what "we" were doing down "here." There I was, the child of empire, clumsily serving as the vessel of Englishness and hopelessly thrown into the field of what seemed to me interminable Anglo-American cultural hostilities.

Power exercised in culture takes devious routes. American writers of great prominence in the American school curriculum and regarded in the academy as Eurocentric and canonical here—in the hands of British imperialist scholars operating overseas in the theater of the empire's Atlantic rim—had suffered a canonical declassification and a technical demotion. Walt Whitman was "potentially a great poet" but lacked "disciplined attention to technique and form"; Eugene O'Neil was "one of the few noteworthy American playwrights"; T. S. Eliot "had given up America for England." Black Americans like Richard Wright, James Baldwin, and Ralph Ellison were emergent writers of the "protest novel" or the "jazz novel." And American women writers? Well, besides Emily Dickinson, no American woman of letters was mentioned at all. In Barbados, we stood in culture not as property owners but as interpreted texts, actors in the shadow of power on the world stage, and pretenders to middle-class status in the postcolony.

Imposed canonical literature, what I call the imperial symbolic, was and is the cultural capital central to the politics of class formation in postcolonial settings like Barbados. In a matter-of-fact way, imperial

cultural form plays a critical role in the elaboration of indigenous aesthetic and social hierarchies and cultural distinctions.

STORY II: T. S. ELIOT AND THE RISE
OF THE POSTCOLONIAL VERNACULAR

Metropolitan canonical cultural form can also serve radical purposes and
be subjected to aberrant decoding and rearticulated within new horizons and fields of possibility. Edward Kamau Brathwaite (1984) tells a
different story of the imperial symbolic than the one I told above. His
story is about the felicitous impact of the canonical high modernist
writer, T. S. Eliot, on the rise of vernacular poetry in the Caribbean.
Again, the moment here is one of hybridity; the medium and conduit
of this improbable connection is one of the most powerful modern car-
riers of hegemonic and counterhegemonic cultural form and wish fulfillment—the phonograph record:

> For those who really made the breakthrough, it was Eliot's actual
> voice—or rather his recorded voice, property of the British Council—
> reading "Preludes," "The Love Song of J. Alfred Prufrock," *The Waste
> Land* and the *Four Quartets*—not the texts—which turned us on. In that
> dry deadpan delivery, the riddims of St Louis (though we didn't know
> the source then) were stark and clear for those of us who at the same time
> were listening to the dislocations of Bird, Dizzy, and Klook. And it is
> interesting that on the whole, the Establishment couldn't stand Eliot's
> voice—far less jazz! Eliot himself, in the sleeve note to *Four Quartets . . .*
> says: "What a recording of a poem by its author can and should preserve,
> is the way that poem sounded to the author when he had finished it. The
> disposition of the lines on the page, and the punctuation (which includes
> the *absence* of punctuation marks . . .) can never give an exact notation of
> the author's metric. The chief value of the author's record . . . is a guide
> to the *rhythms*." (Brathwaite, 1984, pp. 30–31)

The vernacular translations of Eliot's poetry, transacted through the
powerful medium of the phonograph record, connected the canonical
with the everyday and spilled over into the dream of autonomy for
Caribbean letters. Here, in one striking movement, Brathwaite gives
credence to Raymond Williams's thesis in *Culture and Society* (1958) of

the semiautonomous role of culture, its essentially communicative, translatory function across the manichean divide of centers and peripheries. The culture of the third world is therefore the polysemic text of contestatory identities. It is also brimful of the flotsam and detritus of the metropolitan culture industry. Like seasoned bricoleurs, emergent Caribbean writers fished Eliot from a sea of historical ruins and breathed new life into the literary landscape and map of twentieth-century Caribbean cultural form and meaning of style. This was, in the language of Derek Walcott (1993), a "felicitous moment" of hybridity!

STORY III: AFROKITSCH

The play of cultural hybridity in lived and commodified culture is not only produced in the context of third world encounters with Eurocentric cultural form, but is also released in the encounters between the delegitimated cultural forms of marginalized groups such as African American working classes and their third world counterparts in the periphery. Manthia Diawara (1992) tells the story of the powerful impact of African American R&B and soul in late '60s Africa. In this case, the return of diasporic energies from Black America to the African continent unsettles the hegemonic grip of French high culture in the West African neo-colony of Mali. In this context, working-class African American cultural form becomes French-African "cultural capital"; new centers are created in the world and old ones undermined. According to Diawara:

> In 1965, Radio Mali advertised a concert by Junior Wells and his All-Star-Band at the Omnisport in Bamako. The ads promised the Chicago group would electrify the audience with tunes from such stars as Otis Redding, Wilson Pickett, and James Brown. I was very excited because I had records by Junior Walker, and to me, at the time, with my limited English, Junior Wells and Junior Walker were one and the same. (That still happens to me, by the way.) It was a little disappointing that we couldn't have James Brown in person. I had heard that Anglophone countries like Ghana, Liberia, and Nigeria were luckier. They could see James Brown on television, and they even had concerts with Tyrone Davis, Aretha Franklin, and Wilson Pickett.

Sure enough, the concert was electrifying. Junior Wells and his All-Star-Band played "My Girl," "I've Been Loving You Too Long," "It's a Man's World," "There Was a Time," "I Can't Stand Myself," "Papa's Got a Brand-New Bag," "Respect," "Midnight Hour," and, of course, "Say It Loud (I'm Black and I'm Proud)." During the break, some of us were allowed to talk with the musicians and to ask for autographs. The translator for us was a white guy from the United States Information Services. I remember distinguishing myself by going past the translator and asking one of the musicians the following question: "What is your name?" His eyes lit up, and he told me his name and asked me for mine. I said, "My name is Manthia, but my friends call me J. B."—I got the nickname J. B. from my James Brown records.

The next day the news traveled all over Bamako that I spoke English like an American. This was tremendous in a Francophone country where one acquired subjecthood through recourse to *Francité* (thinking through French grammar and logic). Our master thinker was Jean-Paul Sartre. We were also living in awe, a form of silence, thinking that to be Francophone subjects, we had to master *Francité* like Leopold Senghor, who spoke French better than French people. Considered as one who spoke English like Americans and who had a fluent conversation with star musicians, I was acquiring a new type of subjecthood that put me perhaps above my comrades who knew by heart their *Les Chemins de la Liberté* by Sartre. I was on the cutting edge—the front line of the revolution.

You see, for me, then, and for many of my friends, to be liberated was to be exposed to more R&B songs and to be *au courant* of the latest exploits of Muhammad Ali, George Jackson, Angela Davis, Malcolm X, and Martin Luther King, Jr. These were becoming an alternative cultural capital for African youth—imparting to us new structures of feeling and enabling us to subvert the hegemony of *Francité*. (Diawara, 1992, p. 287–288)

Here again, the performativity of culture exceeds its origins. Black America meets West Africa through the circulatory force of the culture industry: records, videos, and music concerts of the stars. There is nothing pure about being black or African. There is nothing original: all is intertextuality, rearticulation, translation. There is no transcendent core: all is epidermis. All is movement in the Black Atlantic. The sound and fury of race signifies everything and nothing.

THE MOVEMENT OF CULTURE

Of course, these processes of hybridity are not exclusively articulated in the periphery. Contemporary developments at late century reveal a return of the subaltern gaze onto "the eye of power itself" (Bhabha, 1994). Huge, dually disorganizing and integrative energies are exerted from the periphery to the center. This is particularly articulated in the movement of masses of third world people to the metropolitan center, bringing new tropes of affiliation and cultural affirmation as well as new sources of tension and contradiction along the lines of race, class, gender, nation, sexuality, and religion. The metropolises of first world societies now struggle to absorb these subaltern subjectivities. State policy and political economies in Europe, the United States, Australia, and Canada now desperately wrestle with the radical challenges and opulent possibilities that the energetic peoples relocated from Africa, Asia, Latin America, and the Middle East present to their newfound homes. In *The Tourist* (1989), Dean MacCannell tracks the new energies of globalization that strike at the heart of old imperial powers, transforming them from within:

Twenty-five years ago the dominant activity shaping world culture was the movement of institutional capital and tourists to the remote regions, and the preparations of the periphery for their arrival. . . . Today, the dominant force—if not numerically, at least in terms of its potential to reshape culture—is the movement of refugees, "boat people," agricultural laborers, displaced peasants, and others from the periphery to centers of power and affluence. Entire villages of Hmong peasants and hunters recently from the highlands of Laos, have been relocated and now live in apartment complexes in Madison, Wisconsin. Refugees from El Salvador work in Manhattan, repackaging cosmetics, removing perfume from Christmas gift boxes, rewrapping it in Valentine gift boxes. Legal and illegal "aliens" weed the agricultural fields of California. The rapid implosion of the "third world" into the first constitutes a reversal and transformation of the structure of tourism. (MacCanell, 1989, pp. xvii)

This tide of mass movement has striking and provocative effects in the realm of culture and literature. It has led, for example, to a virtual transformation of the canons of literature in the center itself. According to Pico Iyer (1993), a new multiperspectival, heterogeneous cultural force is overwhelming and reshaping canonical cultural forms in England and elsewhere:

> The Empire has struck back, as Britain's former colonies have begun to capture the very heart of English literature, while transforming the language with bright colours and strange cadences and foreign eyes. As Vikram Seth, a leading Indian novelist whose books have been set in Tibet and San Francisco, says, "The English language has been taken over, or taken to heart, or taken to tongue, by people whose original language historically it was not." ... The centers of this new frontierless writing are the growing capitals of multicultural life, such as London, Toronto, and to a lesser extent New York, but the form is rising up wherever cultures jangle. (p. 68)

Iyer's observation leads us away from the eruptions of simple-minded nationalisms and the calcified identity politics that rule the political imaginations of our time. For after all, "no race has a monopoly on beauty, on intelligence, on strength/and there is a place for all at the rendezvous of victory" (Aime Cesaire, quoted in Said, 1993, p. 310)

Ultimately, then, who can claim ownership of culture or ethnicity as a final property? The transactions of culture in the modern world forcefully undermine the claim to cultural exceptionalism. Radically underlying the material reality of forces at the center of global capitalism—forces such as colonial domination and racial oppression—are the cultural settlements of what Raymond Williams (1961) calls "The Long Revolution." In the Long Revolution, culture is the alchemy of opposites, the alchemy of classes and races, the point and site of radical hybridity. Culture is also the site of the radical disintegration of biologically derived unities of race, ethnicity, or nation. Culture's polysemic movement constantly challenges the modality of conqueror-conquered or oppressor-oppressed as it undermines, reassembles, and reconfigures long-held traditions, affiliations, and meanings of style into whole new "forms of life." Williams describes this movement of culture in environmental and ecological terms:

> The conquerors may change with the conquered, and even in extreme cases become indistinguishable from them. More usually, a continually varied balance will result. Of the Norman conquest of England, for

example, it is impossible to say that it did not change English society, but equally the eventual result was a very complex change, as can be seen most clearly in the history of the language, which emerged neither as Norman-French nor as Old English, but as a new language deeply affected by both. (1961, pp. 137–138)

Drawing on Williams's insight, and the insights provided by the vignettes of hybridity presented above, I want to talk about race in this book through the prism of culture. In so doing, I seek to promote a rethinking of constructs such as race, identity, and cultural heritage. I argue that the experiences and practices that these concepts seek to summarize are far more dynamic than the ways in which we normally conceptualize them in educational and social science research. I suspect that the dynamism and heterogeneity of the myriad everyday human encounters that produce and reproduce cultures and identities are thwarted in education because even the most radical research continues to be overburdened and weighed down by the legacy of behavioral social science and psychology. Against the latter, much is still measured in the educational field. By contrast, it is in literature and popular culture that the dynamism and complexity of identity, community, and so forth are restored and foregrounded.

Of course, the position I am taking runs up against the current politics of racial identity formation, specifically in the areas of multiculturalism, education, and the politics of curriculum reform. Here, racial understandings underlying the discourse of some multiculturalists and their Eurocentric opponents mark out indelible lines of separation between the culture, literature, and traditions of the West and the culture and traditions of the third world. These highly ideologically charged understandings of identity treat culture as a distinctive form of property that is indisputably owned or possessed by a particular racial group. Indeed, this is one of the symptoms of the racially corrosive heart of human kind that I alluded to earlier.

In *The Uses of Culture*, I refuse the manichean model of racial identity formation. I challenge the glib opposition of the West to the non-West and the curricular project of content addition that now guides the thinking of many of the proponents of identity politics and multicultural reformist frameworks. I specifically look at examples of the complexity and variability of identity formation within the domains of personal autobiography, dominant and subaltern popular culture, and postcolonial literary aesthetics, as well as the so-called canonical traditions of the West. I believe that these sites of popular culture and literary production constitute spaces for the exploration of difference, for interrogating the cultural silence over race and identity in education and society, and for opening up a wide ranging conversation over curriculum reform in the context of the radically diversifying communities we now serve in schools and universities. Throughout this book, I adopt a cultural studies approach to the topic of racial identity formation by foregrounding historical variability, shifting social contexts and environments, and the inevitable trestles of association between the canon and the quotidian, the empire and the postcolony, and suburban and inner-city "realities."

THE CHAPTERS

Throughout this book, I speak with at least two voices. The first is as an intellectual whose formative and perhaps most decisive education occurred in a third world country, the postcolony of Barbados. I am, for better or worse, a child of the empire—an "English rustic in black skin." My other voice is that of an Afro-Caribbean immigrant intellectual displaced to the putative center of the industrial world. I now live in the belly of the beast, a supplicant to a neurotic Uncle Sam. In pursuing this theme of hybridity and duality, I have partially disclosed the agonistic war that wages within the hearts and minds of postcolonial souls, like myself, who inhabit the firmament of the American academy. For whom does the postcolonial intellectual speak? Where is his constituency? Where is his theoretical and political warrant? These themes of incompleteness, duality, and discontinuity are pursued throughout this book, even when I am not writing in an autobiographical mode.

An assertion of the contradictory nature of racial logics is the central thread running throughout the collection of essays brought together here. This is a statement about the potential for ruptures of collective identities that frustrate simplistic projects of racial homogenization and curriculum reform, such as the more mainstream versions of multiculturalism and models of emergent Afrocentrism. Needless to say, *The Uses of Culture*, also stands in critical relief to dominant conceptions of race relations as they are currently presented in Eurocentric school and university curricula programs. I argue in these essays that terms such as "race," "identity," and "culture" are highly decentered and decentering social constructs—the products of historical center-periphery relations and consequent processes of hybridization. The term "center-periphery," here, is not simply to be understood as defining relations between the West and the third world; rather, I wish to call attention as well to contradictions and oppositions within first-world societies such as the United States. A good example of these relations is the current antagonistic dynamic that exists between suburban communities and inner-city residents in the U.S.

A comparative and relational methodological strategy is deployed throughout the book; much attention is paid to cultural reproduction and cultural discontinuity in literary texts, popular culture, and current school curriculum organization. It is important, however, to emphasize that this volume is not intended as a text with an overwhelming master narrative or thesis, nor do I pursue a linear argument or set of arguments from beginning to end. And, *The Uses of Culture* is not organized as a series of chapters that follow an orderly progression, but is a collection of essays that invites the reader to make connections and associations that will emerge when these essays are *taken as a whole*. On the other hand, the resistance to linearity should not be construed to mean that this writer is invested in some New Age relativism. Themes of hybridity, identity, the recoding of race, the project of rethinking multiculturalism, and to get beyond simplistic identity politics repeat themselves throughout the entire text. The book reflects a tortuous search for an understanding of racial dynamics in our contemporary age. It foregrounds an agonized topography—a search that is at once inward and outward, moving through the vast imperial wastes of the postcolony and the opulent fullness of the metropole, through established, canonical culture and the bleeding hearts of contemporary pulp fiction and popular film.

In chapter two, "The Postcolonial Exemplar: The Curriculum in Troubled Times," Wilson Harris and I consider the implications of postcolonial literature as a space for a conversation about establishing a normative basis for communicative action in the curriculum—a communicative action that might get us beyond the implacable categories and particularisms of ethnocentrism in the educational field. I use as an exemplar of this materialist deployment of difference as a humanizing project the work of the Guyanese philosophical novelist, Wilson Harris.

I look at his novel, *The Palace of the Peacock* (1960), and its implications for expanding the conversation over curriculum change in the area of multicultural education.

Chapter three makes the case for the theoretical status of third world popular culture and literature in the analysis of education and social change. Particularly close attention is focused on radical and mainstream sociology of education accounts of "center-periphery relations" in the discussion of first world/third world relationships. Ultimately, the chapter foregrounds ideological struggles that come to be represented in popular cultural texts and practices. I evaluate the extent to which such texts offer possibilities for cultural reproduction or social transformation in education.

In chapter four, I offer a critique of tendencies toward dogmatism and essentialism in current educational theories of racial inequality. I argue that one cannot understand race, paradoxically, by looking at race alone. Different gender, class, and ethnic interests cut at right angles to racial coordination and affiliation. Programmatic reforms that underestimate the powerful role of nuance, contradiction, and heterogeneity within and between racial groups in education are not likely to succeed in either reducing racial antagonism, or assuaging educational inequities. Drawing on the qualitative research on race relations in education of Linda Grant (1984, 1985), Mokubong Nkomo (1984), Michael Omi and Howard Winant (1993), and Joel Spring (1991), I point to the contradictory interests, needs, and desires of minority and majority youth and adults and the subversive role that such competing interests, needs, and desires play in the struggle for race relations reform in education.

Chapter five draws on the theories of identity formation in the writings of C.L.R. James (1978, 1993) and Friedrich Nietzsche (1967). I argue that contemporary film and television play a critical role in the production, coordination, and channeling of suburban resentment and retributive morality onto their central target: the depressed inner city. I also look at the discursive impact of resentment on the sense of capacity and agency among school youth at a comprehensive high school in Los Angeles.

In chapter six, I situate the topic of multicultural education in the context of current debates over Eurocentrism and "Westernness" and the way these discourses are consolidated in the social studies textbooks used in American schools. After advancing a critique of neoconservative educators and their demands for a Western-culture approach to the current crisis in American curriculum and educational organization, I offer my own proposals for educational reform, which I argue can help to facilitate the project of an emancipatory multiculturalism and the fostering of minority cultural identities in the classroom.

Chapter seven connects Richard Herrnstein's and Charles Murray's *The Bell Curve* (1994) to the rise of a medical "panic prose" genre in the 1990s. Here, I draw on the collective insights of my graduate students Ed Buendia, Heriberto Godina, Shuaib Meacham, Carol Mills, Maria Seferian, Theresa Souchet, and Carrie Wilson-Brown. We focus on a degenerative trend in academic writing at late-century in which the line between academic scholarship and pulp fiction has been irrevocably broken by the culture industry. We look at *The Bell Curve* as a special policy document that celebrates white popular wisdom about the problems of the nation pertaining to minorities and the poor. We argue that, like books such as Laurie Garret's *The Coming Plague* (1994) and Richard Preston's *The Hotzone* (1994), and films such as *Outbreak* (1995), *Jurassic Park* (1994), and *Independence Day* (1996), *The Bell Curve* converts the problem of inequality into a problem of biological inadequacy, viral invasion and the like. The task of the suburban professional who is the genuine subject-object of these works is to conduct a massive project of inoculation and elimination. This means, as a practical matter, a disinvestment of government in the poor and the dull and a reinvestment in the wealthy and the brightest.

In the penultimate essay in this volume, chapter eight, I maintain that contemporary educational theorists writing on the topic of racial antagonism have tended to focus too narrowly on sites within the classroom and the school. Insights that could be gained from the study of popular media (television, film, popular music, etc.) and their influence on racial identity formation in education have been forfeited. This state of affairs in contemporary educational research on race is indeed unfortunate as it is ironic. Since media critics, such as Michael Parenti, John Fiske, Len Masterman, and Neil Postman have informed us that the average American schoolchild spends more time watching television than he/she spends in the classroom. I offer a critique of this high/low bifurcation of education and popular culture as the basis for an examination of an emergent phenomenon in the United States: the deep instability of white middle-class identities and the corresponding rise of new ethnic essentialisms reflected in the educational and popular philosophies of Afrocentrism and Euro-panethnicity. Much of the material to be analyzed in this chapter is drawn from contemporary advertising, nostalgia films such as *Forrest Gump* (1994) and *A Time to Kill* (1996), and the idealistic, anti-teacher education pamphlets of Teach for America—the voluntaristic, Ross Perot–inspired youth organization that has as its goal "saving the American inner-city schoolchild." This chapter is intended to open up a new dialogue on the coordinating role that popular culture plays in the production of racial identities.

Finally, chapter nine, "The Uses of Culture," brings the discussion of identity and the limits of ethnic affiliation in education full circle. This chapter foregrounds my collaborative work with Professor Angharad Valdivia and Ph.D. candidate, Nadine Dolby. It argues against the current tendencies to oppose Western culture against the cultures of the non-West, the first world against the third world, and so forth. Drawing on the work of postcolonial authors such as Homi Bhabha, Stuart Hall, and Edward Said, we argue that any single overmastering or ruling identity at the core of the curriculum—whether it be African or Asian or European or Latin American—is in fact a confinement. Such a closed cultural or intellectual system consolidates a kind of illiteracy about one's racial others that is impractical and dangerous in a society in which the demographics of ethnic diversity have outstripped the meaningfulness of a curriculum founded on nineteenth-century principles of ethnic homogenization and the neutralization of difference. No one group has a monopoly on intelligence or beauty. With Dolby and Valdivia, I argue for curriculum reform in the area of race relations founded on the principle of the heterogeneous basis of all knowledge, and the need to find the subtle but abiding links connecting groups across ethnic affiliations and geographical and cultural origins and location. The "Uses of Culture" also serves as an afterword and speaks back to an educational system and a society in danger of being overwhelmed by simple-minded projects of ethnic absolutism.

2

THE POSTCOLONIAL EXEMPLAR
Wilson Harris and the Curriculum in Troubled Times

Proof like Doubt must seek the hidden wound in orders of complacency that mask opportunist codes of hollow survival.

—Wilson Harris, *"A Note on the Genesis of The Guyana Quartet,"* 1985, p. 7

This essay looks at postcolonial literature as a space for the exploration of difference, not simply as a problem, but as an opportunity for a conversation about establishing a normative basis for communicative action in the curriculum. I wish to talk about a communicative action or dialogue that might get us beyond the implacable categories of Eurocentrism and the reductive forms of multiculturalism—beyond the quaint particularisms of the Wild West and the Rest. By invoking postcolonial literature, I point to a redeployment of the vocabulary of difference that might help us to humanize an increasingly commodified, instrumental, and deeply invaded curriculum field. I use as an exemplar of this new materialist humanism (what one postcolonial author calls "the visualization of community" [Gilkes, 1975]) the work of the Guyanese, philosophical novelist, Wilson Harris. I look at his novel, *The Palace of the Peacock* (1960).

Harris's urgings to write began, interestingly, when as a young man, he worked for the Guyanese government as a land surveyor charting the interior of Guyana. Harris reports running around the forests of that South American country reading lots of Hegel and Heidegger. *The*

Palace of the Peacock is a picaresque or quest novel, much like Herman Melville's *Moby Dick,* in which the main characters are pitted against nature in the journey of their lives. But, in Harris's novel, nature is problematized. It is the fecund source of metaphors and allegories about the contested lives of human beings, their oppression of one other, and the open possibilities that reside within collective action, and communal spirit and determination.

THE MOTIF OF POSSIBILITY

> *Our literatures did not passively accept the changing fortunes of their transplanted languages. . . . Soon they ceased to be mere transatlantic reflections. At times they have been the negation of the literatures of Europe; more often they have been a reply.*
>
> —Octavio Paz, *In Search of the Present*—Nobel Lecture 1990, p. 5

> *Some years ago I attempted to outline the possibility of validating or proving the truths that may occupy certain twentieth century works of fiction that diverge, in peculiar degrees, from canons of realism. I sought such proof or validation by bringing the fictions I had in mind into parallel with profound myth that lies apparently eclipsed in largely forgotten so-called savage cultures.*
>
> —Wilson Harris, "A Note on the Genesis of *The Guyana Quartet,*" 1985, p.7

I have come to feel that there are certain words, phrases, and terms that I do not like, even when I am the one using them in my own writing: words and terms such as "origins," "center," "the best," "the brightest," "hierarchy," "pure," "Western," "civilization," even . . . "culture" (although I am sure to use the latter several times before this essay is finished). These words relay and circulate a certain kind of hypocrisy of completeness and self-sufficiency in curriculum theory and design and in the practical matters of everyday human life. Educational theorists and policy makers who invested in these words—these lines of demarcation—now stand clumsily in the doorways of cultural commutation that link human groups to vast underground networks of feeling, sensibility, and promise. Words such as "origins," "Western," and "center" have led us to blocked visions, suspended horizons, and ineluctable retreats. They serve to repress interlocked histories and trestles of association. They paste over the fault lines that have, for some time now, ruptured the undersides of imposed identities deep beneath the glistening surfaces of "Europe," "Africa," "Asia," the "Caribbean," the "Orient," and the "Occident."

So, here we are, almost at the butt-end of the twentieth century, fighting old, stale, atavistic internecine wars in the heart of the curriculum field and in the trenches of educational institutions. I believe it was Henry Kissinger who said that the battles in academic life are as vicious as they are because the stakes are so small. Maybe Old Henry was right, and it is partly our deep investment in words like "center" and "Western" that has gotten us in trouble with our curriculum—our current impasse between the Wild West and the rest of the world. In this new world order, each person grazes on his own grass, so to speak, and in a surrealist sense, turns the key on his own door. These lines of psychic tension and demarcation are powerfully registered in current debates over multiculturalism and curriculum reform. The debaters radically oppose the literature and cultural production associated with the canon to the new literatures of postcolonial writers and indigenous minority novelists and poets. It is assumed by some of the more conservative thinkers, such as William Bennett (1984) and Dinesh D'Souza, that East is East and West is West and never should or must canonical and non-canonical literatures meet in the school curriculum. Some others, more reformist theorists, such as Molefi Asante (1993), assume that since the dominant curriculum thrives on the marginalization of the culture of minorities that minority identities can only be fully redeemed by replacing the Western and Eurocentric bias of the curriculum with non-Western minority literature.

Of course, when talking about this economy of oppositions, one cannot forget the rather unfortunate pronouncements of Fredric Jameson (1986) in an article he published in *Social Text* some years ago entitled "Third World Literature in the Era of Multinational Capitalism." In the article, Jameson asserted that third world literary texts were "necessarily allegorical," and should be read as "national allegories." According to Jameson, third world fiction lacks one critical, historical variable that helps to establish the modern Western realist novel, namely

a radical split between private and the public, between the poetic and the political, between what we have come to think of as the public world of classes, of the economic, and of secular political power: in other words, Freud versus Marx. (1986, p. 69)

Without this split, all third world fiction can be reduced to a single narrative paradigm: "the story of the private individual destiny is always an allegory of the embattled situation of the public third-world culture and society" (p. 65). You can see how far we have come here since Attila the Hun. This is not to say that Jameson's intuitions about third world fiction are entirely off the mark—Harris's work is, after all, deeply allegorical—but Jameson's problems begin when he takes a partial insight and recklessly presses it out into a totalizing usurping epiphany—filling up the periphery and the globe.

I must admit I have reached a kind of exhaustion with a certain usage of the language of difference—a quiet weariness with the language of negation and fatalistic oppositions. This chapter represents a new effort to articulate a motif of possibility—a pragmatics of curriculum that is socially extended, but at the same time deeply invested in the fictive worlds created in postcolonial writing. In these imperfect worlds of imagination, literature leads the way and sociology clumsily follows and, happily, without the burden of "controls." It is an attempt to, in Harris's words, "visualize a community"—a community of lost or broken souls—the community of Donna Haraway's cyborgs, of Gloria Anzaldúa's border people, of Gabriel Marquez's El Macondo, or the folk of Harris's Mariella, dwelling in the interior of Guyana—the mythical rain forests in which the *Cauda Pavonis* or *The Palace of the Peacock* might be glimpsed.[1]

I believe that the challenge of multiculturalism is the critical challenge of curriculum in postmodern times—it is the challenge of living with each other in a world of difference. I believe that postcolonial literature—even more so than postcolonial literary theory and criticism—has sought to foreground this challenge of living in a world of difference in late-century society, and as such, presents us with fictive maps in which power and communication are conceived as operating horizontally, not vertically; not top down as in encoding-decoding, but rhizomatically in the sense that cabalistic passageways link the mighty and the meek on shared and complex terrains. And sometimes, the meek prevail. For example, in Wilson Harris's *The Palace of the Peacock*, tired of abuse, Mariella—Arawak woman and colony—shoots Donne, the colonial oppressor. Her actions are that of a shaman of the folk; the landscape of power is altered in the twinkling of an eye. Donne, we later discover, is that part of the folk reproductive of the old colonial will to power—the colonizer in the colonized—that Mariella as shaman and representative of the folk will redefine. It is within the context of these asymmetrical relations of colonizer and colonized that this literature takes on special significance, but the matter is never straightforward, as we will see Harris's novel.

HISTORICAL FILIATION
OF THE POSTCOLONIAL NOVEL

Of course, the implications of this literature for curriculum cannot be grasped without some attempt to follow its materialist filiations, distributed as they are in the histories of classical and modern colonialism but even more recently, since the '60s, in the footprints scattered across the late-twentieth-century megalopolis—London, Toronto, New York, Paris, Mexico City. These footprints register the presence of the daughters of the dust, the migratory waves of humanity now conquering the West. The state of exile is also the state of rupture of old paradigms, of lost selves, and new affiliations, the locus of emergent self-discovery. In its most compelling forms, postcolonial literature struggles to embrace the old and the new, multiple worlds, divided loyalties, and passionate desires of the Other. As the Sri Lankan writer, Michael Ondaatje puts it in *The English Patient*, this literature celebrates those "nationless . . . deformed by nation states [who] . . . wished to remove the clothing of our countries" (1993, pp. 138–139).

These literary works document the other side of the postmodern—multicultural worlds from which there are no longer exits for retreat. Postcolonial writers are fabricating the new subjects of history and are seeking to install these new subjects within the folds of contemporary imagination. These new subjects are patched together and fitted out with leaky souls. They are flawed or broken human creatures—born in the crucible of cultural modernization, not at all, as some like Roger Kimbal (1990) or Dinesh D'Souza (1991) might argue, stilted prototypes of sociological tracts singing hollow histories of oppression and damnation. And they are not for that matter, as Afrocentric writers like Mike Awkward (1989) might suggest, existing in some prelapsarian past standing up before Adam and Eve.

Emergent postcolonial literatures register a new structure of feeling, of overlapping and cascading epochs of time, of drifting space, free asso-

ciations, of the ample desires and insatiable appetites of the center and
the periphery rolled into one. As such, they offer a new late–twentieth-
century paradigm of curriculum, a kind of poetics of a curriculum
without borders. What we are witnessing at one level is the very transformation of the canons of English, French, and Spanish literatures as
Pico Iyer maintains in a revealing *Time* magazine article:

> Where not long ago a student of the modern English novel would prob-
> ably have been weaned on Graham Greene, Evelyn Waugh and Aldous
> Huxley, now he will more likely be taught Rushdie and Okri and Mo—
> which is fitting in an England where many students' first language is
> Cantonese or Urdu. . . . Thus the shelves of English bookstores are be-
> coming as noisy and polyglot and many hued as the English streets. And
> the English language is being revolutionized from within. Abiku stalks
> us on the page, and triad gangs and "filmi" stars. Hot spices are enter-
> ing English, and tropical birds and sorcerers; readers who are increasingly
> familiar with sushi and samosas are now learning to live with molue buses
> and manuku hedges. (Iyer, 1993, p. 70)

TRANSFORMING THE CANON: WILSON HARRIS AND THE NEW COMMUNITY

And I saw that Donne was ageing in the most remarkable misty way.
                    —Wilson Harris, *The Palace of the Peacock*, p. 49

What might a community of lost or broken souls tell us about curriculum in late-century America? This is the question that Wilson Harris
(1989) poses in his essay, "Literacy and the Imagination," where he suggests that solutions to the problem of literacy in the Americas must
begin with the recognition of the inadequacy of programs of imposi-
tion such as agricultural extension programs and urban literacy projects
that distrust the cultural resources that reside within the masses themselves. In other words, he argues that educators tend to have what he
calls "illiterate imaginations." Harris's observations on literacy point us
in the direction of the resources of the folk—of the popular—the kind
of cultural resources of interpretation and action that Paulo Freire
(1970) discovers in his literacy work with the Brazilian peasants in *Pedagogy of the Oppressed*. And, in another way, this is what Gloria Ladson-

Billings and Annette Henry (1990) have been calling for in their notion of a "curriculum of relevance."

Harris has provided an answer to the problem of "illiterate imaginations" in books such as *The Palace of the Peacock*, *Whole Armour*, *Companions of the Day and Night*, *Da Silva da Silva's Cultivated Wilderness*, and *Genesis of the Clowns*. I want here to focus on *The Palace of the Peacock* as a meditation on a broken community and its set of propositions about a possible reintegration of this community of lost souls. I want to suggest that the way Harris negotiates canonical notions of literary genre, form, characterization, narrative, and social vision has a lot to teach us about the practice of curriculum in the world of difference that has overtaken our social institutions, if not our social consciences. I should say that I turn here to Wilson Harris's *Palace of the Peacock*, but I could have turned to Gabriel Garcia Marquez's *One Hundred Years of Solitude* (1970), or Jamaica Kincaid's *Lucy* (1990), or Salman Rushdie's *Midnight Children* (1981), Ben Okri's *The Famished Road* (1992), Caryl Phillips's *Cambridge* (1992), Michael Ondaatje's *The English Patient* (1992), or Toni Morrison's *Beloved* (1987) or *Jazz* (1992), or, finally, Nawal El Saadawi's *God Dies by the Nile* (1985). All of these novels broadly follow a path of deflation of classical realism of the nineteenth-century novel, and an implosion of an overmastering or ruling narrating subject. Instead, they put in place the angular points of view of a polyglot cast of new characters, protean personalities, and kaleidoscopic visions, open-ended possibilities and journeys from confinement to transformation.

The vast majority of these authors, as Pico Iyer (1993) notes

are writers not of Anglo-Saxon ancestry, born more or less after the war and choosing to write in English [or Spanish or French]. All are situated at the crossroads from which they can reflect, and reflect on new forms of Mississippi Massala of our increasingly small, increasingly mongrel, increasingly mobile global village. Indians writing of a London that is more like Bombay than Bombay, Japanese novelists who cannot read Japanese, Chinese women evoking a China they have seen only in their mothers' stories—all amphibians who do not have an old and a new home so much as two half-homes simultaneously (Iyer, 1993, p. 70).

Where is Wilson Harris to be placed among this motley crew of writers? Well, in some ways, he is a precursor. Like the writers mentioned above, he was "born after the war." But the war that is a point of reference for him is the war that fed the often bitingly satirical poetry of the British war poets, Wilfred Owen, Siegfried Sassoon, and Robert Graves. It is, of course, World War I. Harris was born in Guyana in 1921. He is, as Robert Fraser (1988) tells it, a child of mixed Amerindian, Indian, African, and European blood. He began his professional life as a scientist—a land surveyor—mapping the often tricky interior of Guyana. "Guiana" (Guyana) interestingly is an Amerindian word meaning "land of many waters." Waterfalls abound and many, like the majestic roaring Kaiteur Falls, charge the interior with a sense of terror and sublimity. It is the awesome nature of this terrain that served as an initial inspiration for Harris. Wandering about in the interior of Guyana, Harris spent enormous amounts of time reading Heidegger and Hegel and meditating on time and the psychic dimensions of human life and the way in which the unpredictable and surprising topography of the Guyanese interior landscape seems almost to insinuate itself into the human personality. The rich unpredictability of the Guyana interior in part precipitated his early writings as an imagistic poet of the interior (Fraser, 1988). But most of Harris's work, like *The Palace of the Peacock*, would be written and published in London.

It is the manipulation of imagery, metaphor, and symbol that constitutes the central activity in *The Palace of the Peacock*. The novel, written in 1960, serves a larger purpose of putting to melody a rendezvous with history—a re-encounter between the colonizer and the colonized in different times and places, in multiple personas, in real time, in dream and myth, in life and death. Together, the colonizer and the colonized must share a mutual responsibility for the future which, in the story, can only be glimpsed or constructed after an excruciating revisiting of the past. In the novel, Harris attempts to place twentieth-century humanity in conversation with those who have been designated as the people of "savage cultures." But it is these same savage cultures of the interior of Guyana that support the weight of civilized existence in the coastal suburbs.

To tell a story of this kind, in which multiple cultural systems of interpretations dialogue with each other, Harris must rend the fabric of the classical realist novel. Instead of the fiction of omniscience with its privileged narrator sitting on top of a hierarchy of discourses (see for example, C.L.R. James's *Mariners, Renegades and Castaways* [1978], in which James talks about the bureaucratic deployment of characterization in Herman Melville's *Moby Dick*), Harris produces a form of fiction that, in his own words, "seeks to consume its own biases through the many resurrections of paradoxical imagination and to generate foundations of care within the vessel of place" (1985, p. 9).

The Palace of the Peacock is about the possibility of validating subaltern myths as opposed to colonial accounts of history. In some ways, Harris is saying the folk may yet have the last laugh. For instance, the Caribs of Grenada, it is told in one confrontation with the French, leapt off a mountain to their deaths rather than surrender to the colonizers. The Caribs record this event in myth and folktales in which their ancestors who plunged to their deaths in the seventeenth century ascend to heaven in a flock of stars. On earth, the hill from which they jumped is call *la Morne des Sauteurs* or Leaper's Hill. And at night, presumably, the stars continue to shine down in comment. The stars are in the Carib mythology and astrology the reconstitutions of their broken souls (EPICA Task Force, 1982, p. 9).

The extractable story of Harris's novel takes the form of a journey of reclamation and rediscovery of the colony of Mariella. Mariella is the metaphor for alienated or hidden self—the living resource of the oral traditions of the folk—culture based on use value, outside the exchange relations of commodification. But on board the pontoon that sails up the Cuyuni river in the interior of Guyana are the polyglot broken souls of a subordinating history. Colonizer and colonized must journey, must reach deep into their own souls for new systems of communication that might settle old conflicts. Of course, the quest narrative goes back to the beginning's of the novel: Homer's *Odyssey*, Virgil's *Aeneid*, John Bunyan's *The Pilgrim's Progress*, the great stories of adventure of Geoffrey Chaucer's *Canterbury Tales*, "The Miller," "The Clerk," "Nunnes Priest," and the rest, the extended narrative improvisations and oral documentaries of the African griots—Amiri Baraka's original "Blues People." With the arrival of the modern novel, we have the founding myths of the mariners, renegades, and castaways as C.L.R. James (1978) notes: Daniel Defoe's Robinson Crusoe, Herman Melville's Captain Ahab in *Moby Dick*, and the tormented protagonists of Joseph Conrad's travel fiction, Marlow of *Heart of Darkness*, and Nostromo of *Nostromo*.

But the crew that sets sail on the pontoon in *The Palace of the Peacock*, in a sense represents condensations and fragmentations of these prototypes. The new, imaginary spaces which the characters in this novel inhabit are considerably deflated and impacted—bodies constantly press sensuously against each other. Harris's characters embody the dialectical tensions of self and other, past and present. There is Donne, the tormented captain and leader, who is named after the master of the literary technique of conceit, the metaphysical poet, John Donne. In *The Palace of the Peacock*, Donne is colonizer and agent of dominating instrumental reason, but it is his materialism that blocks his wholeness of being. His abuse of Mariella—Arawak, shaman-woman, and colony—leads to one of his many deaths in the novel. Mariella takes revenge. Donne is also the colonizer's mentality in the colonized who issues decrees: "Donne I suddenly felt in the quickest flash was in me" (p. 33).

Vigilance is the ship's pilot, an Amerindian seer, on whom Donne and the crew must rely for his supersensitive vision to help them navigate and escape the perils lying in the bedrock of the river. There is Cameron the Afro-Scot of "slow feet and fast hands" (pp. 25–26) in pursuit of deep materialistic fantasies—the pork-knocker (the word used to describe a prospector for precious metals in the streams and rivers of Guyana) panning the riverbed for ancestral gold and other precious metals. There is the musical Carroll, an Afro-Carib youth, and player of the Carib bone flute. In his hands, the oar becomes a fully tuned violin. There is Schomburgh, the German-Indian, fisherman and wise uncle to all. There are the Portuguese da Silva twins, at war with themselves and the world, constantly self-contradictory. There is Wishrop, Amerindian (Chinese?), and Jennings the mechanic, Anglo-Saxon married to the folk. And finally, there is Mariella, shaman-woman, ancient yet youthful, as permanent as the stars. She appears in unexpected moments, everywhere, constantly altering the environment and chemistry of associations in the pontoon. Ultimately, Harris tells us this is one spiritually incestuous family that dreamed up their different origins:

> Cameron's great-grandfather had been a dour Scot, and his great-grand-mother an African slave mistress. Cameron was related to Schomburgh (whom he addressed as Uncle with the other members of the crew) and it was well-known that Schomburgh's great-grandfather had come from

Germany, and his great-grandmother was an Arawak American Indian. The whole crew was a spiritual family living and dying together in the common grave out of which they had sprung from again from the same soul and womb as it were. They were all knotted and bound together in the enormous bruised head of Cameron's ancestry and nature as in the white unshaved head of Schomburgh's age and presence. (p. 39)

Unlike the nineteenth-century realist novel of individual psychological interiority, the specific emotions and dispositions of each character are distributed among the other characters in the novel. Donne's superciliousness, can be found expressed in the da Silva twins. He is like the river boy, Carroll, filled with fear and wonder in the face of the majestic waterfall the crew must cross as they take their perilous journey up the river. His craven materialism is reproduced in the obsessed and self-commercial Cameron. These characters on board the shallow pontoon on the journey of their lives are peculiarly flat or hollow entities—broken individuals who need each other to be fully complete. There is no depth or latency to them, they flash on the surface of the novel, and are in some ways "parabolic" characters, to use the language of the West African critic, Emmanuel Obiechina (1978). They introduce a symbolic motif that implicates themselves and the world. Their sharp edges fade and their personalities bleed into each other as the novel progresses. Harris suggests that they are, in fact, one subject of history, one community. We often find it impossible to tell these characters apart. At some point, their individual characteristics are diffused throughout the crew. One gets the picture of a painter furiously experimenting with an expanding rainbow of colors in an infinite palette. Here one is reminded of Peter Greenaway's strobic alternations of light and color in his film, *Prospero's Books* (1991).

Unlike Captain Ahab's Pequod, there is no deck in Harris's novel. These characters are anti-heroes fomented in the belly of the beast—clutching each other in fear and uncertainty as they struggle up river in their shallow pontoon. Nobody is traveling first class here. Their seven-day journey is demarcated by seven deaths, seven dissolutions of the sovereign subject. This journey is, in part, Harris's great effort to recreate the Carib resurrection myth. In Carib mythological structures, human actors have no trouble traveling from life to death and back again, completing a mythical cycle of transformation. Of course, this corridor from life to death is also opened up in Toni Morrison's *Beloved* and *Jazz*, in the filmmaking of Julie Dash in *Daughters of the Dust* (1992), in Jorge Amado's *Dona Flor and Her Two Husbands* (1969) and in the dramatic fables of Derek Walcott in *Dream on Monkey Mountain and Other Stories* (1970).

Harris (1970) also points us to the Renaissance fusion of art and science in the practice of alchemy. The seven-day journey in *The Palace of the Peacock* may thus be compared to the seven stages of the alchemical process during which the *massa confusa* (the *nigredo* or chaos) is immersed (*ablutio*, a stage similar to christian baptism or "death by water") and exposed to a series of chemical and physical changes—through to a stage of purification (*albedo*), to the final *aurum non vulgi* or *Cauda Pavonis* (the peacock's colors) which represents a unity in diversity (this is what the Guyanese critic, Michael Gilkes [1975] calls "the wedding of opposites").

In *The Palace of the Peacock*, the crew exists in the original state of *nigredo* (chaos); their journey through the rapids (*ablutio*) leads to a creative life-in-death transformation, for which Carroll's role as shaman is crucial: "Who and what was Carroll? . . . the living and deadfolk, the embodiment of hate and love, the ambiguity of everyone and everything?" (p. 69). All of this points to a process of inner transformation. Here, again, we see Harris's use of parallel or overlapping time. Carib Resurrection mythology and Renaissance, Egyptian-derived alchemy come together to tell a story of the strange and the familiar in the "infinite rehearsal" of the folk and colonizer in the rivers and forests of the interior of Guyana. The journey up the river and towards the rendezvous with Mariella leads to a series of transformations of the crew in the old pontoon. Each member of the crew is now partially freed from the self-governing, materialistic, and particularistic fantasies that dominated his relationships with his crewmates. This sense of growth in knowledge and understanding is the effect of shared responsibility, mutual liability, and the washing away of implacable masks of sedimented identity and reason. The alchemical vision enlarges to encompass the whole range of objects and persons in the novel. The action unfolds within a decentered and decentering sense of place and context, and the novel builds laterally but always furiously toward a final proliferation of images—fragments cobbled together in the *Cauda Pavonis*. This hollow but latent epiphany which Donne and his crew experience at the top of the rapids as they face their symbolic deaths is a reworking of Odysseus's enchantment, resistance, and partial surrender to the voice of the Sirens—his primitive self and other. Harris breaks through the conventional one-dimensional attitudes and responses to color, light, darkness, touch, smell, sound, and taste that inform our common-sense encounters with each other and the world.

In his essay "On Culture and Creative Drama," Richard Courtney (1988) talks about a resurrection myth associated with the Amerindian peoples. This myth is the creative foundation for Harris's novel:

> Each of these Indian peoples have a major myth which tells how a young hero [heroine] leaves the actual world (dies) and seeks his spirit from whom he obtains "power," returning with it to his village (resurrection) so that he can use this power on the people's behalf. (Courtney, 1988, p. 6)

In *The Palace of the Peacock*, this subaltern or revolutionary power derives from an unflinching self-critique and openness to contradiction, discontinuity, and difference. What Donne and his crew see and experience at the top of the rapid are the tenuous links that connect them to each other and to hidden moral resources within themselves:

> The crew was transformed by the awesome spectacle of a voiceless soundless motion, the purest appearance of vision in the chaos of emotional sense. Earthquake and volcanic water appeared to seize them and stop their ears dashing scales only from their eyes. They saw the naked unequivocal flowing peril and beauty and soul of the pursuer and the pursued all together, and they knew they would perish if they dreamed to turn back. (p. 62)

CONCLUSION

Current debates in multicultural education too easily oppose the literature associated with the canon to the new literatures of minority and indigenous groups, Western civilization to non-Western traditions, and so forth. It is assumed that since the dominant curriculum thrives on the marginalization of the culture of minorities that minority identities can only be fully redeemed by replacing the Western and Eurocentric bias of the curriculum with non-Western minority literature. The work of postcolonial writers such as Wilson Harris directly challenges the easy opposition of the canon to non-Western and third world literature and the curricular project of content addition and replacement that now guides some multicultural frameworks. My point of departure in this chapter follows a theoretical and methodological line of thinking that draws on the historical and genealogical work of Michael Berube (1992), Gerald Graff (1987), and John Guillory (1990), all of whom argue in various ways for a non-canonical reading of the canon. In a strategy complementary to theirs, I have sought to uncover the deep philosophical preoccupations that animate third world writers like Harris in their encounter with master narratives of the West. There is, in fact, in the postcolonial literature a vast project of rewriting that is well on the way—a project I wish to suggest that teachers and students in American schools can no longer remain blissfully ignorant of. Such a project of rewriting guides us toward reading literature both inter-textually and contextually—reading literature "contrapuntally" as Edward Said (1993) suggests. That is to say, we might now read Joseph Conrad's *Heart of Darkness* by the light of Chinua Achebe's *Things Fall Apart*; Daniel Defoe's *Robinson Crusoe* through the eyes of J. M. Coet-zee's *Foe* or Derek Walcott's *Pantomime*; William Shakespeare's *Tempest* under the microscope of George Lamming's *The Pleasures of Exile*; Vir-ginia Woolf's *A Room of One's Own* in concert with Jamaica Kincaid's *Annie John*; and Fyodor Dostoyevsky's *Notes from the Underground* within the knowing gaze of Ralph Ellison's *Invisible Man*.

What I am pointing toward is the need for educators to begin to let the sensibility of a complex, interdependent world into the lives of stu-dents, to challenge the tragic images of mainstream television and text-books, and to expand our own sensibilities in America by embracing the world. Postcolonial literature, it seems, works through a different set of propositions about human actors than the ones that have taken hold in education lately: the origins claims, the centric claims, the West versus the rest, and so forth. These are all tired binarisms that have led to the regimentation of identities—each man turning the key on his own door. The great challenge of our time is to think beyond the para-dox of identity and the other. This is a challenge to rejuvenate linkages of being and association among all peoples in these new times. It is also a challenge to follow the lost steps set in the crosscurrents of history by those dwelling in the light of the *Cauda Pavonis* or the palace of the peacock—the final rendezvous with difference beyond the psychic interior of our human forests.

I believe books like Harris's *The Palace of the Peacock* open up this new terrain in which we find ourselves confronting the other in us. The lost and broken souls of history are asking for a parley that would lead to changing the truths and stabilities of the particularisms now overtaking educational life and the issue of curriculum change.

NOTE

1. It might be helpful for the reader to take a look at some of the following articles and books in which these concepts of subaltern communities are discussed. Donna Haraway (1990) discusses the concept of "cyborg" (or the subaltern, feminist actor who attempts to build communities of resistance across "contradictory worlds" of interests, needs, and desires). See her essay, "A Manifesto for Cyborgs: Science, Technology, and Socialist Feminism in the 1980s," in Linda Nicholson, (ed.), *Feminism/ Postmodernism* (pp. 190–233). New York: Routledge. Gloria Anzaldúa (1987) talks about the people who exist between the colonizer and the colonized—people, who inhabit the "third space" or, in her language, "inhabit both realities" of a colonizing United States and a colonized Mexico (1987, p. 37). See Anzaldúa's (1987) *Borderlands/La Frontera:The New Mestiza*. San Francisco: Spinsters. Gabriel Garcia Marquez's people of "El Macondo" have to negotiate the ruptures generated in the transition from their peasant world to a highly industrialized and modernized context. See for example, Marquez's (1970) *One Hundred Years of Solitude*. New York: Harper and Row. And, finally, Wilson Harris's "Mariella" is both a site of colonial domination and the site of the new identities of the emergent peoples of Guyana and the Caribbean. Mariella is the colonial/postcolonial outpost that is at the center of the narrative of *The Palace of the Peacock*.

3

HOORAY FOR THOSE WHO NEVER CREATED ANYTHING
Popular Culture and the Third World in the Sociology of Education

And my non-fenced island, its brave audacity standing at the stem of this Polynesia, before it, Guadeloupe, split in two down its dorsal line and equal in poverty to us, Haiti where negritude rose for the first time and stated that it believed in its humanity and the funny little tail of Florida where the strangulation of a nigger is being completed, and Africa gigantically caterpillaring up to the Hispanic foot of Europe its nakedness where Death scythes widely.

And I say to myself Bordeaux and Nantes and Liverpool and New York and San Francisco not an inch of this world devoid of my fingerprint . . .

> *oh friendly light*
> *oh fresh light*
> *those who have invented neither powder nor compass*
> *those who could harness neither steam nor electricity*
> *those who explored neither the seas nor the sky but*
> *those without whom the earth would not be the earth.*

—Aime Cesaire, "Return to My Native Land," 1983, pp. 47, 67

This chapter deals polemically with the representation of the third world and the status of third world popular culture and literature in the sociology of education. In what follows, I deliberately set myself in opposition to the subordination of third world people in determinist social theories by reasserting the agency of the oppressed and the decisive importance of popular culture in the ongoing struggle for political sovereignty in the third world. I believe that a radical encounter between current sociology of education and third world literature and popular culture is necessary for new political understandings and for the development of new alliances over the representation of the third world in educational theories, classroom practices, and school texts.

The culture of the differentially oppressed, what I call "popular culture," is still distrusted within contemporary neo-Marxist frameworks and is often theorized as "other" as if "it" floated from afar onto the beaches of unsuspecting theorists. This distrust is pervasive in neo-Marxist accounts of schools and society which systematically subordinate the specific histories and experiences of oppressed women, minorities, and third world people. As an Afro-Caribbean writer, I find myself perhaps permanently out of synch with radical and social science accounts of the human condition which marginalize third world people in this manner.

We are simply deprived of structural positions to speak within the theoretical framework of class essentialist Marxism, or, for that matter, the new wave strategies of periodization associated with postmodernism and poststructuralism now being force-marched into the field of the sociology of education. I have begun to see contemporary Marxism as something of a classical realist text in which the subjective and omniscient speaking positions are reserved for parvenu professional middle-class intellectuals. Much of radical education theory is therefore part of the enabling linguistic competence of a particularly unreflexive community. In these frameworks, third world people are constituted as the specialized objects of radical forms of intellectual tourism (Valdivia, 1995).

In light of this, I wish to point toward a new arena of struggle—the terrain of radical educational and social theory itself. This brings us to the question of who gets to define whom, when, and how? It is fundamentally a question of who gets to generate theory about whom, whose experiences are appropriated, whose theories are considered appropriate, who has privileged access via "Old Boy" or other networks to dominant journals, books, and general circulation. It is also a question of which debates shall have currency within Marxist and neo-Marxist frameworks. It is in this context that I believe that nonsynchronous arguments are long overdue. By invoking the concept of nonsynchrony, I advance the position that individuals (or groups) in their relation to economic, political, and cultural institutions (such as schools) do not share similar needs, interests, or desires at the same point in time.

The concepts of "popular culture" and "difference" have a meaningful centrality in what follows. It is important that I specify their meanings. The term "popular culture" is used throughout in opposition to the essentialist and possessive notion of culture as designating elite art forms, artifacts, and representations. By popular culture, I refer to the historically grounded experiences and practices of oppressed women and men and the processes by which these experiences and practices come to be represented, reconstructed, and reinvented in daily life, in school, in the workplace, and in the news media. In a related sense, I use the concept of "difference" to specify the organizing principles of selection, inclusion, and exclusion that inform the ways in which marginalized third world women and men are positioned and constituted in dominant social theories, social policies, and political agendas.

Much like the classical sociology of Emile Durkheim, Karl Marx, and Max Weber, contemporary center-periphery theories of Philip Altbach (1987), Altbach and Grace Kelly (1978), Martin Carnoy (1974), Andre Gunder Frank (1969), Immanuel Wallerstein (1991), and others have cast third world societies and third world people in terms of overwhelming, totalizing narratives (Said, 1993). In these accounts, third world societies are typically societies without agents—their agency, already siphoned off in the subplots to the main dramas of capitalism, modernism, and imperialism which are played out among the main classes and interest groups in center countries. The men and women of these societies exist absolutely and only in the image and normative gaze of the first world. In radical accounts particularly third world societies are allowed a very narrow set of determinations with respect to a far from benign imperialism—that is, to provide the raw material and the reserve army of labor for a superexploiting capitalism.

This marginalization of the agency of the oppressed is achieved, I wish to suggest, by means of two discursive moves with respect to radical readings of third world relationships to imperialist centers.

The first discursive move in a contemporary radical framework involves a strategy of defining colonialism/imperialism as a total system with a unitary and binding tendency radiating from coordinating centers in Europe or the United States. Cultural practices merely help to flesh out a structuralist economic story of third world/first world encounters. For example, in *Education and Cultural Imperialism* (1974), Martin Carnoy paints a picture of metropole-periphery relations in which the encirclement of third world educational systems is complete:

We hypothesize that the spread of schooling was carried out in the context of imperialism and colonialism—in the spread of mercantilism and capitalism—and, it cannot in its present form and purpose be separated from that context. . . .The structure of schools, since it came from the metropole, was based in large part on the needs of the metropole investors, traders and culture. As we shall show, Western schools were used to develop indigenous elites who served as intermediaries between metropole merchants and plantation labor; they were used to help change social structures to fit in with European concepts of work and interpersonal relationships; and within advanced capitalist economies such as the United States, schools were used to fit white workers and later disenfranchised minorities into economic and social roles defined by the dominant capitalist class. (pp. 15–16)

Altbach and Kelly (1978) are even more definitive and categorical in their evaluation of first world/third world relationships:

The third world is inextricably bound in a network of relationships with the West. Some of these relationships are related to the colonial past, to the sheer economic and technological advantages of industrialized nations and to other "natural" elements in an unequal world. These elements constitute a part of the third world's dependency on the industrialized nations. Such dependency, in many areas at least, is probably inevitable under present conditions. (p. 30)

But even more recent pronouncements, such as those of Immanuel Wallerstein (1991), emphasize the structurally derivative and secondary status of third world economic and political development:

This chain of the transfer of surplus-value frequently (often? almost always?) traverses national boundaries and, when it does, state operations intervene to tilt the sharing among bourgeois towards those bourgeois located in core states. This is unequal exchange, a mechanism in the overall process of the appropriation of surplus-value.

One of the sociogeographic consequences of this system is the uneven distribution of the bourgeoisie and the proletariat in different states, core states containing a higher percentage nationally of bourgeois than peripheral states. In addition, there are systematic differences in *kinds* of bourgeois and proletarians located in the two *zones*. For example, the percentage of wage-earning proletarians is systematically higher in core states. (p. 123)

In none of these accounts is there even a glimmer of recognition of agency or resistance among third world peoples to foreign impositions, nor is there a recognition of the autonomous production of politics or radical alternatives generated by third world women and men in their economic, political, or cultural relationship to the first. Third world economic and cultural institutions are presented as a seamless text on which the face of colonialism and imperialism is securely stamped and etched. There are no traces of indigenous struggles or determinations.

This strategy of totalization allows for a second discursive move toward the suppression of the agency of third world people. Western sociologists of education define the coordinating centers or metropoles as unilaterally setting the structural limits (via sanctions and rewards, evolving systems of domination, and so forth) of third world capacity, maneuverability, political action, and cultural identities. These social theorists, in their accounts of the noneconomic features of imperialism in third world societies, read these off from economic relationships pure and simple. They concentrate only on the formal arenas of education and culture and present third world societies as unitary texts, as bastardized or counterfeit representations of first world countries. Most social scientists writing on the third world hold steadfastly to this monolithic view of the impact of the center on the periphery. Argues Altbach (1987):

> The heritage of colonialism in much of the third world determined the structure of educational systems, the language of schooling, and many aspects of the curriculum. Links to metropolitan centers were imposed during the colonial period and in many cases remain to the present. . . . The curriculum was also patterned on colonial practices, and change was slow. Foreigners had not only directed the educational system, but had determined the meaning of politics and culture as well. (p. 116)

Theories of center-periphery relations such as those advanced above simply underscore the inadequacy of contemporary neo-Marxist and radical sociology of education accounts of imperialist involvement in the third world. Many of these shortcomings can be attributed to the fact that radical educators continue to ignore the critical domains of popular culture and ideology, namely the domains of self-production, representation, racial and sexual oppression, and generally the non-class experiences of struggle and resistance (Cudjoe, 1980). For all intents and purposes, these radical educators remain oblivious to the ways in which third world social actors define for themselves the conditions in which they live.

This poses the question of "the status of the experiential moment in any research" (Hall, 1984, p. 24) on third world educational and social environments. If we are to have a better understanding of the dynamics of domination relations in third world countries as well as a grasp of these dynamics in the peripheries of first world countries (i.e., the oppressed working-class women and men, minorities, and urban poor in the industrial centers of developed countries), then it is crucial that we pay greater attention to the areas of self-production and mobilization in the cultural sphere. This would allow us to theorize and strategize around the fact that heterogeneous forms of domination operating in our societies are maintained and reproduced not simply as the effects of economic structures, but by means of a full-bodied orchestration of difference. The study of popular culture also allows us on the Left to appreciate that oppressed people throw up their own forms of resistance as they encounter structures of domination in their daily lives. This is instanced in the Caribbean in terms of the emancipatory discourses produced in popular music forms such as calypso, dub, and reggae and in women's street theater such as that of the Sistren Theatre Collective of Jamaica (Thomas, 1987). In this regard, the issue of the representation of real, social relations in education and other cultural institutions is of pivotal importance. Pedagogical practices and curriculum materials are—like video, film, television, and rock music— popular cultural "texts" central to both the elaboration of domination and the formation of resistance that counter oppression.

For instance, the maintenance and reproduction of imperialist domination and Western ascendancy since the sixteenth century has been articulated in part, by means of the systematic cannibalization of the dominated peoples of the third world in the mass culture of developed societies. This involves the racialization of the publics of Western capitalist countries and the construction of the women and men of the Latin

America, Africa, Asia, and the Caribbean as the "other" . . . as wholly different. Dawn Gill (1982), in her semiotic analysis of social studies teaching materials used in England in the '80s found that these texts constituted England as a hegemonic public vis-à-vis the third world. The importance of developing countries is defined in terms of what "they" provide for "us." These social studies textbooks provide the following type of narrative: Europeans are constructed as human agents who have organizational ability and are scientific and efficient business people who build roads and railways. Non-Europeans are presented as dependent peoples who have houses and roads built for them and are given jobs which enable them to survive. They are without talent or skills and they are the passive recipients of aid.

Of the twenty-two social studies syllabuses that Gill studied, she found fourteen constructed the third world exclusively in terms of "problems." Typically these problems are presented as internal to developing countries. There is no attempt in these social studies textbooks to critically examine the economic, social, or cultural relationships of developed countries to developing nations. Moreover, these social studies syllabus writers take Western models of development for granted. To "develop" simply means to become more like Britain or the United States. This is what Louis Althusser calls the "mise-en-scene of interpellation" (1971, p. 179)—the way in which the orchestration of cultural form in textbooks and popular culture generates the capacity to speak for whole groups, to arraign these groups, as it were, before a deeply invested court of appeal, draining social life of its history and naturalizing dominant/subordinate relations in the process. This is, by and large, what textbooks do as a matter of course. As Edward Said (1993) points out in his brilliant book, *Culture and Imperialism*, contemporary Western scholars arbitrarily draw down a line between "East" and "West," "West" and "non-West," the "North" and the "South," the "first world" and the "third world." This arbitrary line of demarcation is stabilized by the constant production and reproduction of attributions, differences, desires, and capacities that separate the West from the non-West. The West is rational, the third world is not. The West is democratic, the third world is not. The West is virtuous, moral, and on the side of good and right; the third world is vicious, immoral, and on the side of evil. Indeed, the electronic media images generated around United States' ongoing conflict with Iraq exploits precisely these dichotomies in order to help the

American viewer separate the cause of the U.S. and the West from that of the bad guys of the Middle East—Saddam Hussein and the Iraquis (Kellner, 1993).

It is therefore possible to find in textbooks used in U.S. schools very negative social constructions of the third world. The production and arrangement of images in textbooks draws intertextually on a media language that saturates the popular culture outside and inside the school. More significant than simple stereotyping, then, is the characterization of the relationship of developed countries like the U.S. to third world countries such as Panama and Guatemala in Central America. As the editors (1982) of *Interracial Books for Children Bulletin* maintain in their assessment of textbooks in use in schools across the U.S.:

> Textbooks distort the role of the U.S. in Central America, portraying it only as the perennial "helper." The U.S. has repeatedly intervened in the internal affairs of Central American nations. Rarely are these interventions mentioned. The 34 U.S. military interventions in the area from 1898–1932—and the numerous interventions [once every year and half since WWII], overt and covert, since then—are ignored. (Editors, 1982, p. 5)

A striking example of this kind of vigorous fast-and-loose historical accounting of the United States' relationship to Latin America is illustrated in the misleading treatment many textbooks give to the topic of the overthrow of Jacobo Arbenz's government in Guatemala in 1954. The following passage taken from Thomas Flickema and Paul Kane's *Insights: Latin America* (1980) is typical: "Jacobo Arbenz was the president of Guatemala from 1950 to 1954. While he may not have been a Marxist, he was in favor of them [sic]. Arbenz was defeated, though, before he had a chance to make long-lasting changes in Guatemala." (1980, pp. 106–107) Brief accounts such as this misrepresent history. Arbenz was elected in 1950 by sixty-three percent of the Guatemalan electorate. As Stephen Kinzer wrote in his essay "Isthmus of Violence" in the *Boston Globe Magazine*:

> [In 1954] Jacobo Arbenz won congressional approval for an agrarian program aimed at giving poor Guatemalan peasants access to land for the

first time. Soon after the law was passed, Guatemala's National Agrarian Department began to expropriate the vast unused properties (some 400,000 acres) owned by United Fruit Company. This was too great an outrage for the then Secretary of State John Foster Dulles to accept. Instinctively hostile to Arbenz anyway because of Guatemala's leftist drift, Dulles agreed that the regime would have to be overthrown. Dulles's brother Allen, director of the Central Intelligence Agency, had successfully deposed the government of Iran just a year earlier. He was called upon to duplicate the feat in Guatemala, and he went about the job with gusto. Agents established clandestine radio stations to spread misinformation in Guatemala, American pilots flew unmarked planes that bombed military and civilian targets, and the CIA put together a motley "Liberation Army" of exiles and mercenaries under the control of a disgruntled Guatemalan colonel. President Arbenz was no match for the CIA juggernaut. On June 27, 1954, he resigned. (1981, p. 4)

In contradistinction to this historical account, social studies textbooks present the role of the U.S. almost always as benign, encouraging students to be "shocked" if they hear about anti-American sentiment.

It is striking how these representations of the third world corroborate and reinforce images in the popular culture, particularly in the area of film. Though the treatment of Central America and the third world in social studies textbooks leaves much to be desired, starker examples of the marginalization and the manipulation of difference are reproduced in the popular film culture in the United States. In adventure films such as *Rocky, Red Dawn, Rambo First, Second,* and *Third Blood* and in space operas such as *Aliens, Star Wars,* and *Independence Day,* thousands of alien people die in seconds on the screen and whole cultures are wiped out. American playwright, Rod Clark draws attention to the systematic disorganization of third world cultural identities and the racialization of the American public in the popular film culture. Clark asserts:

No American kid growing up in this country hasn't experienced . . . the phenomenon of watching an old cowboy movie and cheering his head off as the "Indians bite the dust." Sometimes today, when I am depressed at two o'clock in the morning, I turn on the television set and watch bad horror movies all into the morning. What makes me do this? Where do these energies come from? Why do we love movies like *Indiana Jones*? Why do we like space operas like *Star Wars*? It comes from emotional and psychological roots deep in us which are materialized in our economic relationship to the third world, Latin America, and the Caribbean. Imperialism is a deep-seated materialistic fantasy. (Interview with Rod Clark, July 14, 1986)

What Clark suggests here, and what I have maintained all along, is that "difference" is an organizing principle in Western societies which has systematic effects in terms of its function as a prism through which social relations of gender, class, race, and nation are viewed and given meaning and sustenance.

I believe that as educators, cultural producers, critical audiences, and organic intellectuals operating within the university, we can intervene in this discursive field at the critical and strategic points of production and reception. For it is in the creation and consumption of the "products" of popular culture, the generation of school curricula, and the creation of news in the electronic media, that uninstitutionalized experiences are processed and constituted as institutional knowledge and as legitimating cultural symbols that enter the chain of material and social circulation. It is precisely at this conjuncture of education and popular culture that we as radical educators, as public schoolteachers, and third world cultural activists can have important practical and political effects, for herein lie unsuspected opportunities for political theorizing and action. Our project in the classroom might involve, first, submitting these representations of social relations to deconstruction and critique and, second, reassembling new images that reflect our new political understandings of the relationships in which we are embedded.

One vital example makes such a project tangible. The radical curriculum project *El Salvador, the Roots of the Conflict: A Curriculum Guide* (1986) generated by a politically active group of teachers in Oakland, California, challenges dominant representations of Salvadoran people by presenting them as fully realized human beings and as women and men with a legitimate interest in social change and their own self-determination. There are a variety of ways in which this political project of "critical literacy" (Wood, 1985) can be expanded into the community through such vehicles as street theater or community theater. In Jamaica, for instance, groups of working-class women such as the Sistren Theatre Collective have collaborated to use theater as a medium to challenge simultaneously sexual domination and cultural imperialism in their society (Thomas, 1987).

Here, I am not referring to "textual politics" (Belsey, 1980). Developing a non-synchronous political space within education ultimately means dissolving the boundaries between schooling and popular culture. It means conducting what Antonio Gramsci (1983) calls a "war of position" (p. 88) at the same time that we create what Terry Eagleton (1984) identifies as the "critical public sphere" (p. 9). If we are to redress our previous mistake of seeing this sphere as the province of the rising bourgeoisie, we must change our conception of which sites are the strategic areas of struggle. In this way, we can create a language of practical, anti-racist and third world politics that links what is "possibilitarian" (Wexler, 1976) in the humanist and liberal agendas currently existing in some educational institutions to more radical and structural demands for social change. Moreover, by expanding the social welfare logic of the state toward a logic amenable to the needs and desires of the oppressed, we can struggle with the issue of nonsynchrony, social difference, and domination by race, class, gender, and nation.

As a third world speaker, I argue that the method most likely to disarticulate Marxism's economistic, racist, and imperialist reading of education entails listening to the non-synchronous voices from the periphery. This project inevitably means moving away from the current unwarranted privileging of the theoretical and political concerns of the imperial center. To reverse this first world optic in sociological discourses on the third world, I wish to point us in the provocative direction of third world literature and literary theories, to the language of negritude of Aime Cesaire (1983), Franz Fanon (1985), and Leopold Senghor (1981), the Macondo or peasant world of Gabriel Garcia Marquez (1982), Jacques Roumain (1978), and Alejo Carpentier (1979); *The House of Spirits* of Isabelle Allende (1993) and Toni Morrison (1988); and the radical women's geography of June Jordan (1980), Ntozake Shange (1983), and Jayne Cortez (1984). For example, Aime Cesaire (1983) in his "Return to My Native Land" speculates upon the redrawing of national boundaries established in the discourse of imperialist Old World cartography. In the redrawing of the map of the colonial/

postcolonial world, he negates the dialectic of domination between first and third worlds. Asserts Cesaire:

> And my specific geography too; the world map made for my own use, not tainted with the arbitrary colors of scholars, but with the geometry of my spilled blood. . . . For we know now that the sun turns around our earth lighting the parcel designated by our will alone and that every star falls from the sky to earth at our omnipotent command. (p. 77)

By placing the third world in the position traditionally assigned to the first, Cesaire (1983) does not institute a new form of domination—a black power antithesis to white colonialism—rather he suggests a humanized alternative. Cesaire's concept of dominant relationships is rooted in the history of struggle ("the spilled blood"), and thus his reconstruction of the New World goes beyond the abstractions of Western sociology—a sociology that negates the specific histories of third world people. I argue, therefore, that the literature of Cesaire (1983), June Jordan (1980), and others is a literature of resistance (Cudjoe, 1982; Cudjoe and Cain, 1995) which has the explicit effect of decentering the autocratic, ruling first-world subject in third world narratives. In these narratives, third world writers create new sets of social relations and present complex, polysemic, imaginary solutions in their rendezvous with first world domination.

Finally, I seek deliberately to place literature in opposition to sociology, since I believe that in current mainstream and neo–Marxist sociologies the discussion of third world societies are what Michel Foucault (1977) calls "technologies of power" and surveillance (p. 23). I argue for a genuine encounter between third world and New World literature and popular cultural forms and Old World derived sociology of education as the basis of an alternative, radical discourse that would render audible the heterogeneous voices of oppressed, raced, classed, and gendered third world subjects. For as the black feminist poet Ntozake Shange (1983, p. 22) reminds us:

> There is no edge
> no end to the new world
> cuz i have a daughter/trinidad

i have a son/san juan
our twins capetown and palestine/cannot speak the same
language/but we fight the same old men
the same old men who thought the earth was flat
go on over the edge/go on over the edge old men
you'll see us in luanda. or the rest of us in chicago
rounding out the morning/
we are feeding our children the sun . . .

4

CONTRADICTIONS
OF EXPERIENCE
Race, Power, and Inequality
in Schooling

John Robert Ross (1967) tells an anecdote about the American philoso-
pher and educational theorist, William James, that is worth pondering
as we consider the question of theory and race relations in education in
what follows. After a lecture on cosmology and the structure of the
solar system, James was accosted by a diminutive old man.

"Your theory that the sun is the center of the solar system, and that
the earth is a ball which rotates around it, has a very convincing ring to
it, Mr. James but it's wrong. I've got a better theory," contended the
old man.

"And what is that, sir?" inquired James politely.

"That we live on a crust of earth which is on the back of a giant
turtle," said the old man with some relish.

Not wishing to demolish this imaginative little theory by bringing to
bear the masses of scientific evidence which he had at his command,
James decided to gently dissuade his opponent by making him see some
of the limitations of such a theoretical position.

"If your theory is correct, sir," he asked, "what does this turtle stand
on?"

"You are a very clever man, Mr. James, and that's a very good question," replied the diminutive old man, "but I have an answer even to
that question. And my answer is this: the first turtle stands on the back
of a second, far larger, turtle, who directly stands underneath him."

"But what does this second turtle stand on?" persisted James patiently.

To this, the little old man crowed triumphantly, "It's no use, Mr. James—it's turtles all the way down" (Ross, 1967, p. 1).

This little story is broadly relevant to the contemporary situation in the curriculum field in regard to the issue of the status of the conceptualization of the race category and the effects of racial inequality in educational and social life.

The current state of theory with respect to the topic of unequal race relations in education is particularly impoverished (Dyson, 1996; McCarthy, 1995). Contemporary curriculum researchers are still prone to see racial antagonism as a kind of deposit or disease that is triggered into existence by some deeper flaw of individual character or of society ("it is turtles all the way down"). Both mainstream and radical conceptualizations of racial inequality can be described as "essentialist" and "reductionist" in that they effectively eliminate the "noise" of multidimensionality, historical variability, and subjectivity from their explanations of educational differences.

Allow me to clarify what I mean by essentialism and reductionism. By essentialism I refer to the tendency in current liberal and neo-Marxist writing on race and gender to treat social groups as stable or homogeneous entities. Racial groups such as "Asians," "Hispanics," or "Blacks" are therefore discussed as though members of these groups possessed some "unique" or innate set of characteristics that set them apart from "whites." Feminist theorists such as Teresa De Lauretis (1987), bell hooks (1994), and Michele Wallace (1990) have critiqued dominant tendencies to define gender differences in terms of transcendental essences. Wallace, for example, maintains that differences in the political and cultural behavior of minority women and men are determined by social and historical contingencies, not some essentialist checklist of innate, biological, or cultural characteristics. As I will demonstrate, essentialism significantly inhibits a dynamic understanding of race relations and race-based politics in education and society.

Reductionist strategies, on the other hand, tend to locate the "source" of racial differences in schooling in a single variable or cause. Current approaches to racial inequality therefore tend to rely too heavily on linear, mono-causal models or explanations that retreat from the exploration of the political, cultural, and economic contexts in which racial groups encounter one another in schools and society. Carlos Cortes (1986) points to these limitations in his examination of contemporary approaches to racial inequality in education:

> Some analyses [of racial differences in education] have relied too heavily on single-cause explanations. Group educational differentials have been attributed, at various times, to language difference, to cultural conflict, to discriminatory instruments (such as IQ tests), or to the cultural insensitivity of educators. Yet as surely as one of these has been posited as "the," or at least "the principal," cause of group achievement differentials, then other situations are discovered in which these factors exist, and yet group achievement differentials do not occur. . . . There has been a tendency to decontextualize explanations. That is, explanations about the relationship between sociocultural factors and educational achievement often posit causation without consideration of the context in which these factors operate. (p. 16)

As Cortes points out, without an examination of institutional and social context it is difficult to understand how racial inequality operates in education. Current mainstream and radical conceptual frameworks do not effectively capture the heterogeneous and variable nature of race relations in either the school setting or society. Theoretical and practical insights that could be gained from a more relational and comparative method of analyzing racial domination in education—one that attempts to show in detail the links between social structures (whether they be economic, political, or ideological) and what real people such as teachers and students do—have been forfeited.

Despite these limitations, however, the mainstream and radical educational literature on race relations in schooling has pointed us in some very important directions. For instance, we now know where some of the most significant tensions, stresses, and gaps in our current research on social difference and inequality are. I believe that it is precisely these tensions and discontinuities that must be explored if researchers are to begin to develop a more adequate account of the operation of racial inequality in education and society.

In the first part of this chapter, I will examine three areas that I consider crucial points of difference and tension between and within mainstream and radical approaches to racial inequality in the curriculum and educational literature. These areas can be summarized as follows: (a) the structure-culture distinction; (b) macro- versus micro-theoretical and methodological perspectives on race; and (c) the issue of historical variability versus essentialism in the designation of racial categories.

In Part II, I will make the case for an alternative approach to racial inequality, what I shall call a *nonsynchronous theory* of race relations in schooling and society. In advancing the position of nonsynchrony, I will argue against essentialist and reductionist or single-cause explanations of the persistence of racial inequality in education. Instead, I will direct attention to the complex and contradictory nature of race relations in the institutional life of social organizations such as schools.

Let us first look at the principal tensions within mainstream and radical accounts of racial inequality.

I: AREAS OF TENSION IN RACE AND CURRICULUM RESEARCH

Structure Versus Culture

Radical critics such as Michael Apple (1996), Paul Gilroy (1993), and Julien Henriques (1984) maintain that liberal theorists overemphasize "values" as the site of the social motivation for the maintenance and persistence of racial inequality. However, this emphasis on values as a central explanatory variable in liberal theories of racial inequality should not be dismissed out of hand. The primary theoretical and practical merit of this liberal position resides in the fact that it seeks to restore human agency to the project of evaluating the relationship between social difference and education. Thus, for liberal theorists in their examination of racial antagonism in schooling, it is the active agency and subjectivities of students and teachers that really matter and that can make a difference in race relations.

In a related sense, liberal pluralist researchers also recognize the cultural role of education in initiating the social neophyte into dominant values, traditions, and rituals of "stratification" (Durkheim, 1977; Ogbu 1992; Ogbu and Matute-Bianchi, 1986). These researchers conceptualize racial values as emanating from a coherent Cartesian individual subject. When groups or social collectivities are invoked in liberal frameworks on racial inequality, they are specified in terms of aggregates of individuals. The problem here, as I have indicated elsewhere, is that such an emphasis on individual agency also results in the undertheorization of the effectivity of social and economic structures in the determination of racial inequality (McCarthy, 1994).

This tension between structure and agency is also powerfully expressed within radical discourses. Neo-Marxists insist that racial domination must, in part, be understood in the context of capitalism's elaboration of macro-structures, and not simply in terms of individual preferences. They draw our attention to the fact that racial domination is deeply implicated in the fundamental organization of specific human societies, as well as in the evolution of capitalism as a world system (Balibar and Wallerstein, 1991). In this way, we come to understand race as a profoundly social category. Racial domination is thus conceptualized at the level of social collectivities and their differential and conflictual relationships to the means of production. This alerts us to the powerful connections among racial domination and economic inequality, differential material resources and capacities, and unequal access to social and political institutions such as schools.

But recent Marxist cultural criticism has sought to raise other issues concerning social difference and inequality in American education. These issues—identity, subjectivity, culture, language, and agency—direct attention to the informal curriculum of schools and the subcultural practices of school-age youth. This theoretical development has taken place partly in response to the early work of radical school critics, such as Samuel Bowles and Herbert Gintis (1976), who tended to subordinate agency, meaning, and subjectivity to economic structures (for example, the workplace) exogenous to the school. Writers such as Michael Apple (1996) and Henry Giroux (1992) contend that previous neo-Marxist emphasis on economic structures focuses attention on only one part of the puzzle in our investigation of racial inequality. In a similar manner, liberal emphasis on social and cultural "values" as the primary site of racial antagonism provides us with only a partial understanding of the way in which racial dynamics operate. Marxist cultural theorists have accordingly attempted to transcend the binary opposition of structure versus culture entailed in previous neo-Marxist and liberal theories by offering a more interactive view of the central contradictions in capitalist society. However, to the extent that some critical curriculum and educational theorists have attempted to incorporate these more interactive perspectives into their examination of the relationship between schooling and inequality, these efforts have been directed almost exclusively toward understanding the dynamics of class, not race.

Macro–versus Micro–perspectives

There is a further bifurcation in the curriculum and educational litera-ture on race: mainstream theorists have tended to focus more directly on micro-level classroom variables, while radical theorists have offered macro perspectives on racial inequality that have privileged areas out-side the school, such as the economy, the state, and the labor process. Radical school critics have generally specified structural relations at such a high level of abstraction (the level of the mode of production) that all human agency evaporates from their analysis of society. This abstract approach is also residually present in more recent critical cur-riculum studies of social difference and inequality in the institutional settings of schools. (Apple, 1993; Giroux, 1992; Wexler, 1992; Whitty, 1985) These more culturalist theorists have argued that race is linked to other social dynamics, such as class and gender, in a system of multiple determinations. Madan Sarup (1986) has quite persuasively argued that these "additive" models of inequality have simply failed to capture the degree of nuance, variability, discontinuity, and multiplicity of histories and "realities" that exist in the school setting. In a similar manner, both Michael Omi and Howard Winant (1994) and Michael Burawoy (1981) have pointed to the fact that the intersection of race and class can lead, for example, to the augmentation or diminution of racial solidar-ity, depending on the contingencies and variables in a local setting such as the school. All of this underscores the need for theoretical and prac-tical work articulated in what Stuart Hall (1996) calls the "middle range." That is to say, it is important that radical theorists begin to spec-ify more directly the ways in which race operates in the local context of schools.

Let me be clear about what is at issue here. I believe that the radical intuition that racial inequality is implicated and must be understood in the context of the development of capitalism's macrostructures is basi-cally correct if it takes seriously the relatively autonomous workings of the state. This is opposed to the unqualified liberal emphasis on individ-ual motivation and rational action as the terms of reference for "normal" behavior, which locates racism in idiosyncratic, arbitrary, and abnormal attitudes and actions. The latter requires us to abandon materialist explanations of racial antagonism and seek recourse in differential psychology and so on. It places the responsibility for the oppression of racial minorities squarely on the shoulders of these irrational or "authoritarian personalities" (Henriques, 1984). Liberal theorists' reliance on attitudinal models also limits our understanding of social changes in the area of race relations. Within these frameworks, change and transformation of oppressive race relations are made conditional upon the institutional reformation of irrational and intolerant individuals and their return to the observance of rational norms that guide society and its institutions. Needless to say, historical evidence and the very persistence of racial inequality in schools and society go against the grain of this thesis and the programmatic responses it has precipitated. It is insufficient, as neo-Marxist theorists rightly point out, to discuss changing attitudes without addressing structural and institutional impediments in education and society that impede the mobility and maneuverability of racially marginalized groups.

The Issue of History

Though both the macro- and micrological perspectives that underpin radical and liberal formulations give us a general map of racial logics, they do not tell us how movement is orchestrated or realized along the grid of race relations. That is, neither current liberal nor neo-Marxist theories of schooling inform us about the historical trajectory of racial discourse and the struggles over such racial discourse within specific institutions such as education. There is indeed a tendency within mainstream and radical frameworks to treat racial definitions ("black," "white," etc.) as immutable, *a priori* categories (Taussig, 1980). Racial categories such as black and white are taken for granted within the popular common sense as well as in the writings of scholars in the curriculum field. Associated with this tendency are tacit or explicit propositions about the origins of races and racism. Mainstream theorists identify the origin of the races in physical and psychological traits, geography, climate, patterns of ancient migrations, and so on (Gould, 1981; Omi and Winant, 1994). Radical theorists, on the other hand, link race and racism to the specific event of the emergence of capitalism and its "need" to rationalize the super-exploitation of African slave labor and the segmented division of the labor market (Edari, 1984; Harris, 1968; Williams, 1964). The major methodological problem of all of these "origins" arguments is that they presume the eternal existence of racial distinctions and incorporate them into the analysis of racial antagonism as though such distinctions were functional social categories that have remained stable throughout history. In both mainstream and radical writings, then, "race" is historically given. (After all, says our common sense, "we know who black people and white people are merely by observation and inspection.") The historical variability associated with racial categories and the social purposes that racial distinctions serve are consequently undertheorized.

But, as Omi and Winant (1994) have argued, race is preeminently a social historical concept. For example, it is only through developed social practices and the particular elaboration of historical and material relations in the United States that "white consciousness," with its associated category "white people," emerged. Likewise, it is only through similar historical and social practices that racial "others"—who in reality have varying economic and social positions—emerged under the definitions of "black," "Asian," "Latino," and so on. In this sense, racial categories "have varied widely from decade to decade. The variation both reflects and in turn shapes racial understanding and dynamics. It establishes often contradictory parameters of racial identity into which both individuals and groups must fit" (Omi and Winant, 1994, p. 3). A few examples are useful in helping to illustrate the instability and variability of racial categories.

In the United States, the racial classification "white" evolved with the consolidation of slavery in the seventeenth century. Euro-American settlers of various "ancestries" (Dutch, English, and so forth) claimed a common identity in relation to exploited and enslaved African peoples. As Winthrop Jordan observes:

> From the first, then, vis-à-vis "Negro" the concept embedded in the term *Christian* seems to have conveyed much of the idea and feeling of "we" against "they": to be *Christian* was to be civilized rather than barbarous, English rather than African, white rather than black. The term *Christian* itself proved to have remarkable elasticity, for by the end of the seventeenth century it was being used to define a species of slavery which had altogether lost any connection with explicit religious difference. In

the Virginia code of 1705, for example, the term sounded much more like a definition of race than of religion: "And for a further christian care and usage of all christian servants, Be it also enacted, by the authority aforesaid, and it is hereby enacted, That no Negroes, mulattos, or Indians, although christians, or Jews, Moors, Mahometans, or other infidels, shall, at any time, purchase any christian servant, nor any other, except of their own complexion, or such as are declared slaves by this act."

By this time "Christianity" had somehow become intimately linked with "complexion". . . . Most suggestive of all, there seems to have been something of a shift during the seventeenth century in the terminology which Englishmen in the colonies applied to themselves. From the initially most common term *Christian,* at mid-century there was a marked shift toward "English" and "free." After about 1680, taking the colonies as a whole, a new term appeared—"white." (1968, pp. 94–95)

It is through these same practices of inclusion and exclusion that the "others" of colonial America—the enslaved African peoples—were defined as "Negro" or "black." Thus, the racial category "negro" redefined and homogenized the plural identities of disparate African people whose "ethnic origins" were Ibo, Yoruba, Fulani, and so on.

Racial categories also vary contemporaneously between societies. For example, while the racial designation "black" in the United States refers only to people of African descent, in England, oppressed Asian and Afro-Caribbean minorities have appropriated "black" as a counter-hegemonic identity. In Latin America, racial categories are used and appropriated with a higher degree of flexibility than in the United States. Omi and Winant (1986), drawing on the work of cultural anthropologist Marvin Harris (1968), foreground this variability and discontinuity in race relations in Latin America:

By contrast [to the United States], a striking feature of race relations in the lowland areas of Latin America since the abolition of slavery has been the relative absence of sharply defined racial groupings. No such rigid descent rule characterizes racial identity in many Latin American societies. Brazil, for example, has historically had less rigid conceptions of race, and thus a variety of "intermediate" racial categories exist. Indeed, as Harris notes, "One of the most striking consequences of the Brazilian system of racial identification is that parents and children and even brothers and sisters are frequently accepted as representatives of quite opposite racial types." Such a possibility is incomprehensible within the logic of racial categories in the U.S. (p. 61)

Social practices of racial classification are elaborated and contested throughout society and within given institutions by personal and collective action. In this way, racial definitions are reproduced and transformed. Historically, education has been a principal site for the reproduction and elaboration of racial meaning and racial identities—an examination of racial discourses within the overall trajectory of curriculum and educational theories and practices rapidly disabuses us of the notion that education is a "neutral" or "innocent" institution with respect to racial struggles (JanMohamed, 1987; JanMohamed and Lloyd, 1987). An investigation of the genealogy of racial discourses in education would, for example, take us through the domains of:

1. Colonial/plantation America's education laws that prohibited the education of black Americans, such as the eighteenth-century statutes of South Carolina and other states (JanMohamed and Lloyd, 1987, p. 7).
2. Jim Crow educational policies in the North and the South, and the segregation and concentration of blacks and other minorities into inferior schools (Carnoy, 1974; Ogbu, 1978; Ogbu and Matute-Bianchi, M. 1986).
3. Measurement of mental capacities and human intelligence theories— from the laboratory of cranium estimates to the anthropological and biological theories of racial difference in the work of Samuel George Morton (1839) and Arthur Gobineau (1915), and the genetics-based theories of race and intelligence of Arthur Jensen (1969, 1981, 1984) and Richard Hernstein and Charles Murray (1994).
4. Curriculum theories of social efficiency, differential psychology, and cultural deprivation that labeled black youth as "underachievers," and consider black families and black communities as "defective" and "dysfunctional" (Reed, 1992).
5. Liberal and progressive-inspired educational programs, such as Head Start, compensatory education, and multicultural programs that have been aimed at helping to close the educational and cultural gap between black and white youth.

At every historical juncture of the racialization of dominant educational institutions in the United States, African Americans and other racial minorities have contested and have sought to redefine hegemonic conceptions of racial differences in "intelligence" and "achievement" and the curriculum strategies of inclusion, exclusion, and selection that these commonsense racial theories have undergirded. Over the years, this cultural resistance has been mobilized on two principal fronts. On the one hand, since the period of Reconstruction, African Americans have conducted what Gramsci would call a "war of manoeuver" outside the "trenches" of dominant universities, schools, and other educational centers by establishing parallel and alternative institutions of learning (Gramsci, 1971). While it is true that these institutions have not always been directed toward transformative projects, black educational institutions have provided a material basis for the nurture of black intellectual and cultural autonomy (Marable, 1985; West, 1993).

At the same time as alternative institutions were expanded, African Americans and other minorities conducted a "war of position" (Gramsci, 1971, p. 88) in the courts and the schools for equal access to education. These struggles have also been enlarged to include insurgent challenges over a redefinition of dominant university academic programs. These challenges have directly influenced the emergence of the "new" disciplines of ethnic studies, women's studies, and so on, that have helped to broaden the range of knowledge and interests in the university setting.

Education has played a central role in the drama of struggles over racial identities and meaning in the United States. But any historical account of the racialization of American education must avoid the easy familiarity of linear narrative. The reproduction of hegemonic racial meanings, the persistence of racial inequality, and the mobilization of minority resistance to dominant educational institutions have not proceeded in a straightforward, coherent, or predictable way. A systematic exploration of the history of race relations in education does, however, lead us to a recognition of the agency of oppressed minorities, the fluidity and complexity of social dynamics, and the many-sided character of minority/majority relations in education.

The tensions and silences within mainstream and radical approaches to racial inequality discussed here underscore the need for a more relational and contextual approach to the operation of racial differences in school-ing. Such an approach would allow us to understand better the complex operation of racial logics in education and would help us to explore more adequately the vital links that exist between racial inequality and other dynamics—such as class and gender—operating in the school setting.

In the next section, I will present two related alternative approaches—the theories of *parallelism* and *nonsynchrony*—that will directly address the conceptually difficult but intriguing issues concerning (a) the structuration and formation of racial difference in education, and (b) the intersection of race, class, and gender dynamics in the institutional setting of schools. I will also report and discuss ethnographic examples of nonsynchrony in race relations in school from the work of Linda Grant (1984), Mokubong Nkomo (1984), and Joel Spring (1991).

II: NONSYNCHRONY AND PARALLELISM: LINKING RACE TO GENDER AND CLASS DYNAMICS IN EDUCATION

Racial inequality is a complex, many-sided phenomenon that embraces both structural and cultural characteristics. But exactly how does racial difference operate in education? How are the "widely disparate circumstances of individual and group racial identities" (Omi and Winant, 1986, p. 169) intertwined and mediated in the formal and informal practices of social institutions such as schools? How do educational institutions "integrate" the macro- and micro-dynamics of difference? One of the most significant contributions to understanding these difficult questions regarding the operation of racial inequality has been advanced by Michael W. Apple and Lois Weis (1983) in what they call the "parallelist position." This approach, the authors argue, is useful to conceptualize the social formation in terms of interlocking spheres of economy, politics, and culture. Apple and Weis further claim that dynamics of race, class, and gender interact with each other in complex ways, but that each is necessary for the mutual reproduction of the others. It is impossible to give these arguments the thorough going treatment that they deserve in this chapter. Perhaps the most significant contribution of the parallelist approach is that it introduces into the sociology of curriculum a way to understand causation in respect to racial antagonism. Proponents of parallelism suggest that causal processes related to racial antagonism should not be located in a single theoretical space—namely, the structural properties of "the" economy. They conceptualize causal influences on racial antagonism as coming from a "plurality" of processes operating simultaneously within the economic, cultural, and political spheres of society. The parallelist approach problematizes the elements of positivistic causal linearity that residually percolate within radical accounts of race and curriculum. In this sense, too, proponents avoid the tendency toward single-cause explanations of racial inequality dominant among adherents of mainstream neo-correlational paradigms of educational research. Instead, these theorists point us toward the plurality of liabilities that handicap minority youth as raced, classed, and gendered social subjects. Accordingly, Apple and Weis (1983) maintain the following:

> First, rather than a unidimensional theory in which economic form is determinate, society is conceived of as being made up of three interrelated spheres-economic, cultural/ideological, and political.
>
> Second, we need to be cautious about assuming that ideologies are only ideas held in one's head. They are better thought of less as things than as social processes. Nor are ideologies linear configurations, simple processes that all necessarily work in the same direction or reinforce each other.... A number of elements or dynamics are usually present at the same time in any one instance. This is important. Ideological form is *not* reducible to class. Processes of gender, age, and race enter directly into the ideological moment [in] daily life. (p. 24)

Apple and Weis also criticize the tendency of mainstream and radical theorists to bifurcate society into separate domains of structure and culture. They argue that such arbitrary bifurcation directly helps to consolidate tendencies toward essentialism and reductionism in contemporary thinking about race. Researchers often "locate the fundamental elements of race, not surprisingly, on their homeground" (Omi and Winant, 1986, p. 52). For neo-Marxists, then, it is necessary first to understand the class basis of racial inequality; and for liberal theorists, cultural and social values and prejudices are the primary sources of racial antagonism. In contrast, Apple and Weis contend that race is not a "category" or a "thing-in-itself," but a vital social process which is integrally linked to other social processes and dynamics operating in education and society. The proposition that "each sphere of social life is constituted of dynamics of class, race, and gender" (Apple and Weis, 1983, p. 25) has broad theoretical and practical merit. For example, it highlights the fact that it is impossible to understand fully the problem of the phenomenally high school–dropout rate among black and Latino youth without taking into account the lived experience of race, class, and gender oppressions in U.S. urban centers and the ways in which the intersections of these social dynamics work systematically to "disqualify" inner-city minority youth in educational institutions and in the job market. Similarly, a theoretical emphasis on gender dynamics helps to complement our understanding of the unequal division of labor in schools and society and directs our attention to the ways in which capitalism uses patriarchal relations to depress the wage scale and the social value of women's labor.

In advancing the parallelist position, Apple and Weis therefore present us with a theory of *overdetermination* in which the unequal processes and outcomes of teaching and learning and of schooling in general are produced by constant interactions among three dynamics (race, gender, and class) and in three spheres (economic, political, and cultural). In significant ways, it represented a major advance over the "single group" and single variable studies that had previously dominated the study of race relations in education.

However, the parallelist approach to the analysis of social difference, while rejecting much of the reductionism and essentialism of earlier neo-Marxist structuralism, offers an "additive" model of the intersection of race, class, and gender that does not address issues of contradiction and tension in schooling in systematic way. Neither does it address the "mix" of contingencies, interests, desires, needs, differential assets and capacities that exist in local settings such as schools. Thus, it does not offer us a clear enough insight into the specificity or directionality of effects of the intersection of race, class, and gender in education.

In contrast to the parallelist theorists' emphasis on reciprocity and mutuality of effects, I will argue that the intersection of race, class, and gender in the institutional setting of the school is systematically *contradictory* or *nonsynchronous* and can lead to the augmentation or diminution of the effect of race, or for that matter, any other of these variables operating in the school environment. Since the terms *contradiction* and *nonsynchrony* are central to the arguments about the operation of racial inequality and antagonism in education, it is important that I specify their meanings.

The term contradiction is used here and throughout in two senses. First, the use of contradiction is associated with a deconstructive project that is central to my discussion of racial inequality in this essay. I therefore draw attention to moments of rupture, discontinuity, and structural silence in existing school practices and the social relations that define minority/majority encounters in education. For example, those moments of discontinuity and contradiction are articulated in the gap between the ostensible objective of efficiency in school policies such as tracking and their unintended effects of marginalizing a large number of minority youth from an academic curriculum. Although educational administrators and teachers readily point to the "fairness" of existing normative rules and criteria for assigning students to high/low academic tracks in school, the application of such normative rules (grades, standardized tests, etc.) procedurally constrains black access to genuine equality of opportunity in education. At the same time, these rules benefit white middle-class youth, who have a clear advantage in instructional opportunities, teacher time, and material resources such as computers (Gamaron and Berends, 1986; Oakes, 1992).

In all-black schools, similar structural advantages can accrue to black middle-class students vis-à-vis their working-class counterparts, as Ray Rist (1970) discovered. These "built-in" discontinuities exist as structuring principles in everyday pedagogical and curriculum practices and profoundly influence minority encounters with whites in education. There is also a second, more positive application of the term "contradiction." In this more Hegelian usage of the concept, I wish to suggest that it is precisely these discontinuities in minority/majority experiences in schooling that can provoke or motivate qualitative change and forward motion in social relations between blacks and whites. In this sense, I maintain that a genuine exploration of these contradictions in minority/majority education can help to lay the foundation for meaningful race-relations reform.

The concept of nonsynchrony also highlights the issue of contradiction, but, more specifically, summarizes the vast differences in interests, needs, desires, and identity that separate different minority groups from each other and from majority whites in educational settings. Like Hall (1996), I believe that it is necessary to offer theoretical arguments at a more conjunctural or middle level if we are to better understand the way these dynamics operate in schools. Such an emphasis on nonsynchrony in the institutional context would help us to specify these dynamics of race and gender in a manner that would allow for an understanding of the multivocal, multi-accented nature of human sub-jectivity and the genuinely polysemic nature of minority/majority rela-tions in education and society.

By invoking the concepts of contradiction and nonsynchrony, I wish to advance the position that individuals or groups, in their relation to economic, political, and cultural institutions such as schools, do *not* share identical consciousness, nor express the same interests, needs, or desires "at the same point in time" (Hicks, p. 221). With this connec-tion, I also attach great importance to the organizing principles of selec-tion, inclusion, and exclusion that deeply inform curriculum and credentialing practices in schools. These principles operate in ways that affect how marginalized minority youth are positioned in dominant social and educational policies and agendas. Schooling in this sense con-stitutes a site for the production of politics. The politics of difference is a critical dimension of the way in which nonsynchrony operates in the material context of the school and can be regarded as the expression of "culturally sanctioned, rational responses to struggles over scarce [or unequal] resources" (Wellman, 1977, p. 4).

As we will see, students (and teachers) tend to be rewarded and sanc-tioned differently according to the resources and assets they are able to mobilize inside the school and in the community. This capacity to mobilize resources, and exploit the unequal reward system and sym-bolic rituals of schooling, varies considerably according to the race, gender, and class backgrounds of minority and majority students. White middle-class male students come into schools with clear social and eco-nomic advantages and in turn often have these advantages confirmed and augmented by the unequal curriculum and pedagogical practices of schooling. However, this process is not simple, and the production of inequality in school is a highly contradictory and nonsynchronous phe-nomenon—one that does not guarantee nice, clean, or definitive out-comes for embattled minority and majority school actors.

But exactly how does nonsynchrony work in practice? What are the "rules of the game" that govern the production of inequality in the school setting, and how does inequality in educational institutions become specifically classed, gendered, or raced?

There are four types of relations that govern the nonsynchronous interactions of raced, classed, and gendered minority and majority actors in the school setting. These relations can be specified as follows:

(1) *Relations of competition*: These include competition for access to educational institutions, credentials, instructional opportunity, financial and technical resources, and so on.

(2) *Relations of exploitation*: The school mediates the economy's demands for different types of labor in its preparation of young people for the labor force.

(3) *Relations of domination*: Power in schooling is highly stratified and is expressed in terms of a hierarchy of relations and structures—administration to teacher, teacher to student, and so forth. The school also mediates demands for symbolic control and legitimation from a racial and patriarchal state.

(4) *Relations of cultural selection*: This is the totalizing principle of "difference" that organizes meaning and identity-formation in school life. This organizing principle is expressed in terms of cultural strategies or rules of inclusion/exclusion or in-group/out-group that determine whose knowledge gets into the curriculum, and that also determine the pedagogical practices of ability grouping, diagnosing, and marking of school youth. These relations also help to define the terms under which endogenous competition for credentials, resources, and status can take place in the school. It should be noted that there is considerable overlap between and among the relations of cultural selection and the other relations of competition, exploitation, and domination operating in the everyday practices of minority and majority school actors.

In the school setting, each of these four types of relations interact with, define, and are defined by the others in an uneven and decentered manner. For example, the principles of cultural selection embodied in codes of dress, behavior, and so forth, which help to determine the assignment of minority youth to low-ability groups, also help to position these youth in respect to power (domination) relations with majority peers and adults (Grant, 1984; Rist 1970). Cultural selection influences minority access to instructional opportunity as well as access to opportunities for leadership and status in the classroom and school (Gamoran and Berends, 1986).

Similarly, cultural selection helps regulate endogenous competition for credentials and resources, thereby constraining minority and majority students to a differential structure of "choices" with respect to the job market and, ultimately, to the differential exploitation of their labor power by employers. The reverse is also true in that teachers' and administrators' perceptions of the structure of opportunities for minorities (exploitation relations) can have a significant impact on the processes of cultural selection of minority and majority students to ability groups and curricular tracks in schooling (Sarup, 1986; Spring, 1991; Troyna and Hatcher, 1992). By virtue of the daily operation of these four types of relations—competition, exploitation, domination, and cultural selection—and their complex interaction with dynamics of race, class, and gender, schooling is a nonsynchronous situation or context. In this nonsynchronous context, racial dynamics constantly shape and are in turn shaped by the other forms of structuration, namely, gender and class.

The concept of nonsynchrony begins to get at the complexity of causal motion and effects "on the ground," as it were. It also raises questions about the nature, exercise, and multiple determination of power within that middle ground of everyday practices in schooling. The fact is that dynamic relations of race, class, and gender do not unproblematically reproduce each other. These relations are complex and often have contradictory effects in institutional settings. The intersection of race, class, and gender at the local level of schooling can lead to interruptions, discontinuities, augmentations, or diminutions of the original effects of any one of these dynamics. For example, while schooling in a racist society like the United States is by definition a "racist institution," its racial character might not be the dominant variable shaping conflict over inequality in every schooling situation (Hall, 1981, p. 68). That is to say that, (a) the particular mix of history, subjectivities, interests, and capacities that minority and majority actors bring to the institutional context, and, (b) the way in which these actors negotiate and "settle" the rules of the game (the relations of competition, exploitation, domination, and cultural selection) will determine the dominant character and direction of effects in the specific school setting. The "dominant" character, then, refers to the relations along which "endogenous differences" in the school are principally articulated.

These dominant relations thus constitute an "articulating principle," pulling the entire ensemble of relations in the school setting into a "unity" or focus for conflict (Laclau and Mouffe, 1985). Such an articulating principle may be race, class, or gender. For instance, it can be argued that a sex-dominant situation exists within American university education with respect to struggles over women's studies and the very status of women in academe itself. Gender has been the articulating principle that has sharpened our focus on issues around the fundamental operation of white male privilege in the university system with respect to the differentiated organization of curricular knowledge, unequal patterns of selection and appointment to tenure-track faculty positions, unequal relations between male professors and female students, and so on. The issue of gender has had multiple effects, illuminating flash points of difference across a range of traditional male-dominated disciplines. Sexual antagonism within academe has focused our attention on the modus operandi of the university and its relations of competition, exploitation, domination, and cultural selection.

The powerful impact of sexual antagonism within the university system has also had the effect of masking racial antagonism and/or determining the political terms on which racial conflicts may be fought. (One should hasten to note that the opposite was true in the '60s, when the balance of forces of protest accentuated racial difference as the articulating principle for conflicts over inequality in education.) Issues of minority failure and the under-representation of minorities at every level within the tertiary section of American education continue to be peripheral to the dominant Anglocentric agenda in the university system. Figure 1. illustrates the interaction of race, gender, and class relations in a sex-dominant situation. In this model of nonsynchrony, relations of sexual antagonism and solidarity are augmented, while race and class relations are diminished. The principal sources of conflict, mobilization, and counter-mobilization within given educational institutions may then be centered around issues of gender relations: sexual harassment, women's studies, new codes of conduct within the university governing relations between the sexes, and so forth. This might not necessarily mean that racial issues are entirely ignored. Indeed, one result might be that issues concerning minority women and their interests would become more directly strategic and pivotal in the overall effort to secure reform in race relations in education—a situation in which it could be said that race-relations struggles benefited from a heightened focus on gender issues. (Clearly, the reverse was true in the '60s.)

In recent sociological and educational literature, there are a number of practical examples of the contradictory effects of the intersection of race, class, and gender in settings inside and outside schools that help to illustrate the nonsynchronous model I have outlined above.

The work of researchers such as Omi and Winant (1986, 1994) and Madan Sarup (1986) directs our attention to the issues of nonsynchrony and contradiction in minority/majority relations in education and society and suggests not only their complexity, but the impossibility of predicting the effects of these dynamic relations in any formulaic way based on a monolithic view of race. In their discussion of educational and political institutions, Omi and Winant and Sarup have emphasized the fact that racial and sexual antagonisms can, at times, cut at right angles to class solidarity. The work of Manning Marable (1985) and Joel Spring (1991) focuses our attention in the opposite direction by pointing to the way in which class antagonisms have tended to undermine racial solidarity among minority groups involved in mainstream institutions. For instance, Marable and Spring both argue that since the civil rights gains of the '60s, there has been a powerful socioeconomic and cultural division within the African American community. This has been principally expressed in terms of the evolution of an upwardly mobile black middle class, which has sought to distance itself in social, educational, and political terms from an increasingly impoverished

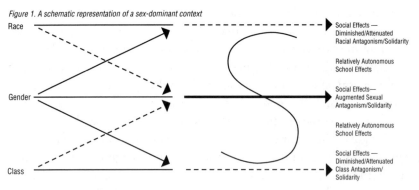

Figure 1. A schematic representation of a sex-dominant context

Race — Social Effects — Diminished/Attenuated Racial Antagonism/Solidarity

Relatively Autonomous School Effects

Gender — Social Effects— Augmented Sexual Antagonism/Solidarity

Relatively Autonomous School Effects

Class — Social Effects — Diminished/Attenuated Class Antagonism/ Solidarity

A schematic representation of the intersection of dynamics of race, gender, and class in schooling (S). in which gender is responsible for the most powerful effects in the school setting.
Strong lines indicate autonomous effects.
Double strong lines indicate augmented effects.
Broken lines indicate attenuated/relatively autonomous or diminished effects.

black underclass. Spring contends that such class antagonism operates as a determining variable in critical relationships between the black community and mainstream educational institutions. As we shall see, such class antagonism also influences and is influenced by the endogenous relations of differentiation that already exist within the school setting.

As a case in point, Spring (1991) reports on a longitudinal study of the class dynamics operating within a black suburban community ("Black Suburbia") and the way in which these dynamics are expressed in the relationship of black students and their parents to the school system. Spring's account begins in the mid-1960s, when a black professional middle-class (PMC) population moved into a Midwestern suburb formerly populated predominantly by whites. The new residents of Black Suburbia quickly embraced the predominantly white-administered school system, and, as the constituents of the "new" middle class in the district, black PMC parents and their children readily granted legitimacy to the existing relations of differentiation (cultural selection, competition, etc.) operating in the schools in exchange for access to "quality education." They saw the schools as guarantors of continued upward mobility for their children. According to Spring:

> A study of the community [Black Suburbia] in the late 1960s showed the mobility concerns and educational aspirations of the new black population. . . . The study found that both the middle-aged and young middle-class black residents had high expectations of upward mobility and believed that *quality* schools were a major element in *quality* community. The population group labeled "New, Middle-Aged, Black Middle-Class Residents" were earning more than $10,000 a year and were employed as managers, proprietors, and professionals. This group was found to have an "extraordinarily high degree" of expectations for continuing upward mobility and concern about the quality of schools. (1991, pp. 122)

The term "quality school" indeed summarizes an ideological and strategic trade-off or "settlement" that was tacitly implicated in the overwhelming black PMC support for the white-administered school system. But this settlement between the school system and its new PMC patrons was soon to be imperiled by a change in the demographic and cultural milieu of the Black Suburbia community and its schools.

Both the expectations of upward mobility and the high educational aspirations of the black PMC residents who had arrived in the late '60s were, by the '70s, "threatened by the rapid influx of a poor black population" (p. 123). This influx of low-income blacks dramatically altered the social-class composition of Black Suburbia: "Between 1970 and 1973 the percentage of children from welfare families increased ... from 16 to 51 percent. In other words, the migration of upwardly mobile middle-class blacks was followed by the rapid migration of black welfare families" (p. 123).

Teachers responded negatively to the entrance of increased numbers of low-income black students into the school system, and the "standard of education" in Black Suburbia schools declined:

> One of the first things to happen was that the educational expectations of the mainly white teachers and administrators in the school system began to fall. This seemed to be caused by the assumption of the white school staff that the blacks moving into the community were not interested in education and would create major problems in the school system (p. 123).

These developments precipitated a crisis of legitimacy in the school system's relations to its black constituents. However, the racial response of the school system to the increasing numbers of black students was not met or challenged by a united front among the residents of Black Suburbia. Indeed, class antagonism between the more affluent blacks and the lower-class black residents intensified both in the schools and in the community. PMC black students blamed the lower-class students for the sharp decline in educational standards in the schools. They complained that the teachers were incapable of controlling the "rowdies"—a code word for low-income black students. This class antagonism spilled over into the community. Many black PMC parents expressed the fear that their children would be corrupted by the "rowdy-culture" of welfare kids who "were organized into natural street groupings," as one parent put it (p. 125). As class antagonism intensified, the more affluent black parents took the further step of withdrawing their children from the public schools and sending them to private institutions. Quite simply, black PMC parents lost confidence in the public schools because they perceived teachers as having failed to control the "corrupting" influence of low-income students, whom these parents blamed along with their teachers for the declining standard of education.

From the perspective of these PMC black residents, the Black Suburbia school system had failed to deliver on its side of a tacit agreement, and black students stood to suffer in competitive relations for credentials and long-term futures in the labor market. According to Spring's account, the racially motivated strategies of cultural selection in Black Suburbia schools now had, as a response to the influx of low-income students, come full circle to handicap black middle-class youth as well. Ultimately, in this highly provocative racial situation, the response of the residents of Black Suburbia to their school system was highly contradictory and nonsynchronous. Racial dynamics and identity were clearly "dominated" by class interests. To say the least, the interests of black PMC residents and their low-income counterparts diverged. Resulting class antagonism undermined racial solidarity among black residents and weakened their collective ability to negotiate with the white-administered school system or challenge the racial basis of the poor-quality education that the public schools were offering to their children.

Mokubong Nkomo (1984), in his discussion of the dynamics of race/class relations in the South African educational system during the apartheid regime, describes quite a different example of a nonsynchronous racial situation. In this case, Nkomo asserts that the enormous constraints placed on the aspirations and economic futures of black students and the blatant Afrikaner ideological domination of black universities had unintended effects nonsynchronous with the interests of the apartheid state.

In South African Bantu universities, both black students from urban PMC backgrounds and working-class students from the Bantustans experienced high levels of cultural alienation. This alienation strengthened the bonds of racial solidarity between these youth of different class backgrounds. Racial solidarity among black students was certainly not a policy goal of the South African government prior to the recent Mandela regime. For instance, in the late 1950s, the apartheid government sought to balkanize South African black youth by creating highly restrictive, ethnically segregated universities in the Bantustans. The Afrikaner regime attempted to maintain existing relations of racial domination and exploitation of South African blacks by pursuing a policy of "separate development." In the area of higher education, this policy of balkanization meant, for example, that student enrollment at the University of Zululand was limited exclusively to the Zulu and Swazi ethnic groups. And while, prior to the late '50s, Indians and "coloreds" could go to the University College of Fort Hare, the 1959 Transfer Act restricted enrollment at this college to Xhosa-speaking Africans only (Nkomo, 1984).

The clear intent of such divide-and-conquer policies of the South African government was to promote the intensification of intra- and inter-ethnic differences among Africans, Indians, and "coloreds" as a means of disorganizing the political capacities and the collective will of the subordinated racial groups in South Africa. Nkomo informs us that the South African state's domination of black universities went even further. Through the Department of Bantu Education, the state directly controlled curriculum content, student admissions, academic staff appointments, and finances of black universities. This state control was peculiar to the Bantu universities, since the "European" universities in South Africa enjoyed and continue to enjoy academic autonomy in consonance with the Western tradition.

It was precisely this intense racialization of the South African state's relationship to the black universities and its coercive attempt to consolidate relations of domination in these educational institutions that led to a radical incongruity between black students' aspirations and the official university establishment. These contradictions and frustrations within the apartheid Bantu educational system provoked a critical consciousness among urban PMC black students and their less privileged counterparts from the Bantustans, bringing them together in a common struggle against the apartheid system. This development was not without a touch of irony: Bantu universities created by the South African government as part of the apartheid structure and developed to facilitate exploitation by undermining political alliances among black South African youth had the unintended effect of galvanizing powerful cultural resistance and racial solidarity against the apartheid system. Indeed, these Bantu universities had been among the principal sites of racial mobilization and struggle against apartheid in the 1980s and the early '90s.

The example of the black South African university illustrates a race-dominant nonsynchronous situation. As Nkomo demonstrates, racial solidarity and its obverse, racial antagonism, constituted the dominant principles along which unequal social relations in these Bantu universities were ordered, organized, and culturally expressed—this, despite the significant economic and social class divides that existed and continue to exist among black South African students.

A final example brings us closer to the nonsynchronous dynamics of unequal social relations in a number of classrooms in the United States. Based on findings from a study of "face-to-face interactions" in six desegregated elementary school classrooms in a Midwestern industrial city, Linda Grant (1984) concludes that "Black females' experiences in desegregated schools . . . differ from those of other race-gender groups and cannot be fully understood . . . by extrapolating from the research on females or research on blacks" (p. 99). Grant conducted detailed observations of the classrooms of six teachers (all women, three blacks and three whites) at the two schools, Ridgeley and Glendon, involved in her two-year study. Some 40 percent of the 139 students in the first-grade classrooms studied were black. Among other things, Grant found that strategies of evaluation and cultural selection (tracking, ability grouping, and so forth) varied considerably according to "race-gender group" (black males, black females, white females, and white males). For instance, black females were more likely than any other race-gender group to be labeled "non-academic" (p. 102). This was particularly true of the evaluations by white teachers:

> White teachers, however, gave more attention to non-academic criteria. In fact, they made proportionally fewer comments of an academic nature about black girls than any other race-gender group. [For example,] assessments of black females contrasted markedly with these teachers' assessments of white males, for which academic criteria predominated. (p. 102)

While teachers identified both black and white females as more mature and "helpful" than their male counterparts, white girls were more likely to be labeled as "cognitively mature and ready for school" (p. 102). In contrast, black girls were labeled as "socially mature," and Grant contends that teachers exploited this "social maturity." Teachers' strategies of cultural selection also had an impact on domination relations of teacher to student and student to student in these first-grade classrooms. Thus, teachers tended to deploy black girls as "go-betweens" when they wanted to communicate rules and convey messages informally to black boys. Race-gender group differences were also reproduced in terms of the first graders' access to instructional opportunity, as well as in the students' informal relations and orientation to teachers in the Ridgeley and Glendon elementary schools:

> Although generally compliant with teachers' rules, black females were less tied to teachers than white girls were and approached them only when they had a specific need to do so. White girls spent more time with teachers, prolonging questions into chats about personal issues. Black girls' contacts were briefer, more task related, and often on behalf of a peer rather than self. (p. 107)

Black males were even less likely than black females—or any other race-gender group—to have extended conversation with teachers, and relations between black males and their female teachers were defined by mutual estrangement. Grant suggests in another article based on the same data that these teachers were, in fact, afraid of or "threatened" by their black male students. Nevertheless, teachers tended to identify at least one black male in each class whom they singled out as an academic achiever or a "superstar" (Grant, 1985). In none of the six elementary school classrooms that Grant studied were any of the black girls singled out as high academic achievers. Instead, Grant maintains, black girls were typified as "average achievers" and assigned to "average" or "below average" track placements and ability groups.

Ultimately, the effects of the processes of cultural selection that obtained in the classrooms that Grant observed were nonsynchronous. Teachers did not relate to their black students or white students in any consistent or monolithic way. Gender differences powerfully influenced and modified the differential ways in which teachers evaluated, diagnosed, labeled, and tracked black and white students, and again, the influence of gender on the racial response of teachers to their students was particularly evident in the case of black females. Teachers emphasized the social, caring, and nurturing qualities of the black females in their first-grade classrooms, and, in subtle ways, teachers encouraged them to "pursue social contacts, rather than press towards high academic achievement" (1984, p. 103). Consequently, Grant concluded that desegregated education at the elementary schools she studied had unintended negative (racial) costs for all black children. The processes of cultural selection that occurred in the desegregated classrooms she observed worked to the disadvantage of black children in terms of successful competition for instructional opportunity, teacher time, and resources in these schools. Grant also suggests that existing processes of cultural differentiation not only served to constrain the structure of educational opportunity available to black students within the school setting, but also helped to structure their incorporation into exploitative relationships from the very beginning of their school careers. For black females, these negative effects were particularly severe and strongly gender determined. This meant that black girls' experiences in the six desegregated classrooms were systematically nonsynchronous or qualitatively different from those of black boys or any other race-gender group:

> The emphasis on black girls' social rather than academic skills, which occurs particularly in white-teacher classrooms, might point to a hidden cost of desegregation for black girls. Although they are usually the top students in black classes, they lose this stature to white children in desegregated rooms. Their development seems to become less balanced, with emphasis on social skills. . . . Black girls' everyday schooling experiences seem more likely to nudge them toward stereotypical roles of black women than toward [academic] alternatives. These include serving others and maintaining peaceable ties among diverse persons rather than developing one's own skills (p. 109).

CONCLUSION

The findings of curriculum and educational researchers such as Grant, Nkomo, and Spring help to illustrate and clarify the complex workings of racial logics in the highly differentiated environment that exists in school settings. By drawing attention to contradiction and nonsynchrony in the educational processes of cultural selection, competition, exploitation, and domination, these critical researchers directly challenge mainstream single-group studies of inequality in schooling. While mainstream studies have tended to isolate the variable of race from gender and class, the work of Grant, Spring, and Nkomo underscores the need to examine the historical specificity and variability of race and its nonsynchronous interaction with forms of class and gender structuration in education. Monolithic theories of racial inequality suppress such an understanding of these complexities and treat racial groups as biological and cultural "unities" (Hall, 1989; 1996). The nonsynchronous approach to the study of inequality in schooling alerts us to the fact that different race-class-gender groups not only have qualitatively different experiences in schools but actually exist in constitutive tension, often engage in active competition with each other, receive different forms of rewards, sanctions, and evaluation, and are ultimately structured into differential futures. The critical theoretical and practical task is, then, as Hall suggests, one of "radically decoding" the specific relations and nuances of particular historical and institutional contexts:

> One needs to know how different groups were inserted historically, and the relations which have tended to erode and transform, or to preserve these distinctions through time—not simply as residues and traces of previous modes, but as active structuring principles of the present society. Racial categories *alone* will *not* provide or explain these. (Hall, 1980, p. 339)

The work of Grant, Nkomo, Spring, and Sarup has furthered our understanding of the complex workings of race and other dynamics in educational institutions. Their findings help us to deconstruct the multiple determination of power in the school setting and the way in which such micro-politics can undermine the viability of conventional approaches to curriculum reform. What is abundantly clear is that monolithic or homogeneous strategies of curriculum reform that attempt to ignore or avoid the contradictions of race, class, and gender at the institutional level will be of limited use to minority youth. New approaches to race relations reform in education must begin with a more sophisticated and robust conceptualization of the dynamic relations between minority and majority actors in the school setting. Efforts to get beyond essentialism, reductionism, and dogmatism in current theories of race relations in education are a good place to start. The multifaceted nature of race relations and its role in education and society requires a many-sided response—one that recognizes that minorities are not simply oppressed as racial subjects, but are positioned as classed and gendered subjects as well. These dynamics of race, class, and gender are interwoven unevenly into the social fabric of American institutions in the educational system, the economy, and the state.

This uneven interaction of race with other variables, namely class and gender—a process that I have called nonsynchrony—is a practical matter that defines the daily encounter of minority and majority actors in institutional and social settings. For example, the experience of educational inequality for a black middle-class youth is qualitatively different from that of a black working-class girl from a female-headed household. As we saw in the case of Spring's report on Black Suburbia discussed earlier, black middle-class youth had more material options than their working-class peers when the racially motivated inferior education in Black Suburbia's public schools became intolerable. The parents of these middle-class youth pulled them out of the public school system and placed them in private educational institutions. Black working-class youth did not have this maneuverability—their parents could not afford to pull them out of the racist public school system.

These issues of nonsynchrony shape and structure the experience of inequality and the micro- and macro-dynamics of educational and social life and must be factored into any broad-ranged strategy for an alternative approach to race-relations reform. What, then, are the elements of a nonsynchronous interactive approach to race and educational reform?

To begin with, I wish to acknowledge that we are in a specific historical conjuncture in the evolution of race relations in the United States—one in which racial antagonism and evidence of increasing minority disadvantage in education and the economy are prominent features of social life (Apple, 1996; Hacker, 1995; Kozol, 1992) . We must, however, resist facile solutions to these problems. Even more critically, we must avoid the temptation to respond to the problem of racial inequality in an undifferentiated and essentialist manner. Essentialist and reductionist approaches to race typically ignore or flatten out the differences within minority groups, while at the same time insulating the problem of racial inequality from issues of class and sexual oppression. In the past, while such reformist approaches to racial inequality have benefited a small, upwardly mobile element of the minority population, significant sections of that community (particularly inner-city youth and lower-class minority women and men) have been by-passed.

However, the emergent theory and practice of nonsynchrony must not merely be negative in its implications. It is not enough to critique existing theoretical and programmatic approaches to race and educational reform. The articulation of a nonsynchronous perspective entails a second, more positive conceptual and practical task: to stake out a field within contemporary debates on schooling for a more inclusive, affirmative politics that takes seriously the differential needs, interests, and desires of minority women and men and urban working-class youth. This positive theoretical and practical intervention in current educational debates involves the affirmation of alternative political, cultural, and ideological practices that help to define the identity and efficacy of subordinated groups.

For example, it is important to assert that the very cultural differences in language, history, and subjectivity that dominant educators have diagnosed as minorities' "symptoms of inadequacy" can be re-read transformatively as constituting alternative practices that are radically opposed to the dominant culture (JanMohamed and Lloyd, 1987, p. 10). Indeed, it is precisely these marginalized themes of minority agency, language, and cultural identity that black feminist writers such as Zora Neale Hurston, June Jordan, and Ntozake Shange have mobilized into a powerful insurgent discourse that challenges current stereotypical representations of minority people reproduced in the dominant American literature and popular culture. It is also these issues of cultural identity, language, and difference that have historically defined minority struggles in education for community control and alternative schooling.

Of course, in affirming the positive moment in minority history and struggles in the United States, a nonsynchronous perspective should not fall back on the idea of race as some essentialist expression of language and cultural solidarity. Neither should we rush headlong into the politics of cultural exceptionalism or the "the celebration of cultural diversity for its own sake" (JanMohamed and Lloyd, 1987, p. 10). Rather, racial difference must be understood as one of a variety of starting points for drawing out the various solidarities among subordinated minorities, women, and working-class youth over our separate but related forms of oppression. In this way, we also move beyond tendencies to treat "race" as a stable, measurable deposit or category. Racial difference is, therefore, to be understood as a subject-position that can only be defined in political terms—that is in terms of the effects of economic exploitation, political disenfranchisement and cultural and ideological repression. In this respect, discourses on education and racial inequality cannot be meaningfully separated from discourses on issues of police brutality in black neighborhoods, or the sexual and mental harassment of minority women on the shop floor. We also come to recognize that examining race relations is critical not only to understand social life as it is expressed in the margins of society, but ultimately, for an understanding of life as it is expressed in the broad political and economic mainstream of this country. For, as Hall maintains:

> If you try to stop the story about racial politics, racial divisions, racist ideologies short of confronting some of these difficult issues; if you present an idealized picture of a "multicultural" or "ethnically varied" society which doesn't look at the way racism has acted back inside the working class itself, the way in which racism has combined with, for example, sexism working back within the black population itself; if you try to tell the story as if somewhere around the corner some whole constituted class is waiting for a green light to advance and displace the racist enemy ... you will have done absolutely nothing whatsoever for the political understanding of your students. (1981, p. 68)

5

READING THE AMERICAN POPULAR
Suburban Resentment and the Representation of the Inner City in Contemporary Film and Television

INTRODUCTION

This essay runs contrary to contemporary mainstream and some radical theories of race and popular culture that tend to place television, film, and advertizing outside the circuits of social meanings at some self-constituting point from which these technologies then exert effects on a differentiated mass public (Parenti, 1992; Postman, 1986). In what follows, I take a decidedly cultural studies approach to the discussion of the role of contemporary tools of simulation—television and film—in the production and reproduction of contemporary race relations. I situate these social technologies within the turmoil of contemporary life as cultivators and provokers of racial meanings and common sense. I see television and film as fulfilling a certain bardic function, singing back to society lullabies about what a large cross section and hegemonic part of it "already knows."

Like Richard Campbell (1987), I reject the vertical model of communication that insists on encoding/decoding. I am more inclined to theorize the operation of communicative power in horizontal or rhizomatic terms. Television and film, then, address and position viewers at the "center" of a cultural map in which suburban, middle-class values "triumph" over practices that drift away from mainstream social norms. In this arrangement, the suburb, in the language of Christopher Lasch

(1991), becomes "The True and Only Heaven": the great incubator and harbinger of neo-evolutionary development, progress and modernity in an erstwhile unstable and unreliable world. Our suburban dweller is the great philosophical and semiotic meta-subject of daytime and nighttime radio talk shows, television evening news, and tabloid hysteria. He is our contemporary Sweeney Erectus, our last rational man, standing on the pyres of resentment. "Suburban dweller" here refers to all those agents travelling in the covered wagons of post-sixties white flight from America's increasingly black and brown, increasingly immigrant, urban centers. White flight created settlements and catchment areas that fanned out farther and farther away from the city's inner radius, thereby establishing the racial character of the suburban-urban divide (Wilson, 1994). As taxed-based revenues, resources, and services followed America's fleeing middle classes out of the city, a great gulf opened up between the suburban dweller and America's inner-city resident. Into this void, contemporary television, film, and popular culture entered, creating the most poignantly sordid fantasies of inner-city degeneracy and moral decrepitude. These representations of urban life would serve as markers of the distance the suburban dweller had travelled away from perdition. Televisual and filmic fantasies would underscore the extent to which the inner-city dweller was irredeemably lost in the dystopic urban core. Within the broad vocabulary of reproductive technologies at its disposal, the preference for the medium shot in television tells the suburban viewer "We are one with you," as the body of the television subject seems to correspond one-for-one with the viewer.

As Raymond Williams (1974) argues in *Television: Technology and Cultural Form*, television, film, advertising, and textbooks are powerful forces situated in cultural circuits themselves—not outside as some pure technological or elemental force or some fourth estate, as the professional ideology of mainstream journalism tends to suggest. These are circuits that consist of a proliferation of capacities, interests, needs, desires, priorities, and commitments—fields of affiliation and fields of association.

One such circuit is the discourse of resentment, or the practice of defining one's identity through the negation of the "other." This chapter will focus on this discourse in contemporary race relations and point to the critical coordinating role of news magazines, television, the

Hollywood film industry, and the common sense of black filmmakers themselves in the reproduction and maintenance of the discourse of resentment—particularly its supporting themes of crime, violence, and suburban security. I also consider the discursive impact of resentment on the sense of capacity and agency among black school youth at a comprehensive high school, Liberty High, in Los Angeles. For this segment, I will draw on ethnographic data collected at this Los Angeles high school some six months before the videotaped images of LAPD's police beating of Rodney King reverberated around the world.

Drawing on the theories of identity formation in the writings of C.L.R. James (1978, 1993) and Friedrich Nietzsche (1967), I argue that the electronic-media play a critical role in the production and channelling of suburban anxieties and retributive morality onto its central target: the depressed inner city. These developments deeply inform race relations in late-century society. These race relations are conducted in the field of simulation as before a putative public court of appeal (Baudrillard, 1983).

STANDING ON THE PYRES OF RESENTMENT

I feel deadly faint, bowed and humped, as though I were Adam, staggering beneath the piled centuries since Paradise.

—Ahab in Herman Melville's *Moby Dick* 1851, p. 535

These words, uttered in a moment of crisis in the nineteenth-century canonical text of Herman Melville's *Moby Dick*, might well have been uttered by Michael Douglas as D-fens in the contemporary popular cultural text of *Falling Down* (1993), or Douglas as Tom Sanders in the anti-feminist, proto-resentment film, *Disclosure* (1994). Douglas is the great twentieth-century suburban middle-class male victim, flattened and spread out against the surface of a narcotic screen "like a patient etherized upon a table" (Eliot, 1964, p. 11).

In two extraordinary texts written in the late forties, *Mariners, Renegades, and Castaways: The Story of Herman Melville and the World We Live In* (1978) and *American Civilization* (1993), C.L.R. James made the provocative observation that American popular cultural texts—comic strips, popular film, popular music, soap opera, and the detective novel—offered sharper intellectual lines of insight on the contradictions and tensions of modern life in postindustrial society than the entire corpus of academic work in the social sciences. For James, comic strips such as *Dick Tracy* and popular films such as Charlie Chaplin's *Modern Times* (1936) and John Huston's *The Maltese Falcon* (1941) were direct aesthetic descendants of Melville's *Moby Dick*. These popular texts removed the veil that covered social relations in the twentieth century "too terrible to relate," except in the realm of fantasy and imagination (Morrison, 1990, p. 302).

In a remarkable way, popular culture was for James the great storehouse of twentieth-century integrative energies, desires, and frustrations—freely mingling the quotidian with the extreme, the mundane with the horrific, didactic moral values with their prurient undersides, the aesthetic with the grotesque. With one brush stroke, James drew a direct line of connection between the canonical work of writers like Melville and the operation of meaning and values in contemporary popular cultural forms. For James, these popular texts foregrounded the rise of a new historical subject on the national and world stage. This subject was a projection of the overrationalized and overdetermined modern industrial age. This new subject was a resentment-type personality who articulated an authoritarian populism: the mutant, acerbic and emotionally charged common sense of the professional middle class (Douglas with a satchel of hand grenades in *Falling Down*, Harry and Louise of the anti-health care reform ads). This authoritarian personality was, in James' view, willing to wreck all in the hell-bent prosecution of his own moral agenda and personal ambition. According to James, what was unusual and egregious about the resentment personality type in *Moby Dick* and the nineteenth-century world of Melville had become pseudonormative by the time of *The Maltese Falcon* in the '40s—a period marked by the rise of what James called "nonchalant cynicism" (James 1993, p. 125).

In *The Maltese Falcon* (1941), detective Sam Spade (Humphrey Bogart), gets to put the woman he loves in jail for the murder of his corrupt partner, Miles Archer. Their love is overridden by the ideology of professionalism and the socionormative priority of making wrongdoers pay. As the paranoid Spade says plaintively to his lover, "I don't like the idea that you'd played me for a sucker." In this version of game theory, there are no free riders. Loafers are persona non grata. In Sam Spade's case, lovers do not have any special privileges beyond the domestic sphere. Spade is playing by his own ethics and chucking human relations and feelings as encumbering eruptions of irrationality. This is a tart dish of public common sense. He is the eternal stand in or proxy for middle-American values. Spade holds the line against the threat of invasion by the morally corrupt other, the socially different, the culturally deviant and deprived. The bad guys kill and the good guys kill too; but the good guys kill more efficiently. Morality is on the side of the technologically and materially endowed. The fun and games of law and order are, therefore, part of a deeply ethnocentric, gendered and class-based system of difference—a hierarchy of priorities in the world we live in. It is a game of exclusions intended to preserve the safety of the suburban domestic space. In popular culture, the public sphere becomes the site of distorted communication and social anxieties and prejudices. By combining detective and gangster rolled into one transcendent subject, Spade enters into the semiotic field, simultaneously, as suburban plaintiff and libidinal cruiser.

Contemporary popular discussion of crime and violence also follows this logic of closed narrative where the greatest fear is that the enemy will be let into our neighborhoods, and the greatest stress on public policy may be how to keep the unwanted off the taxpayer dependent welfare rolls and out of our town, safely in prisons, and so forth. Sam Spade's worries have had a meltdown in our time, and they have become a potent, paranoid resentment-brew that spills over from the fantasy land of television and film into the real world in which we live.

What James's astute comments point us toward is the fact that the filmic and televisual discourse of crime and violence is not simply about crime or violence. Art is not here simply imitating life in some unthinking process of mimesis. Art is productive and generative. Televisual and filmic discourses about crime and violence, as Gerbner (1970) and others argue, are fundamentally urban fables about the operation of power and the production of meaning and values in society. They are about moral re-evaluation, about our collective tensions, crises, and fears. They are about how America as a society deals with the social troubles that afflict its soul: sexism, racism, and the like. In this sense, popular culture—the world of film noir and the B movie, of tabloids, and the mainstream press—constitutes a relentless pulp mill of social fictions of transmuted and transposed power. At late-century, Sam Spade has been replaced by the towering popular and preternatural intelligence of Sweeney Erectus, our guide into the moral inferno. James wrote almost prophetically about resentment mutations and the time lag in the modern in the late forties. The aim of this chapter is to describe the operation of resentment a half century later in our time—a time in which racial antagonism has been the host to a parasitic resentment stoked by the media and circulating in popular culture.

DANGEROUS ZONES

The crisis of the middle class is of commanding gravity. . . . The crisis is hardening the attitude of the middle class toward the dependent poor, and to the extent that the poor are urban and black and Latino and the middle class suburban and white, race relations are under a new exogenous strain. . .

—Jack Beatty, 1994, p. 70

Recently, *Time* magazine published two articles that together document the rise of contemporary suburban middle-class resentment. In these articles, crime and violence are fetishized, transmuted in the language of the coming invasion of the abstract racial other. Together, the articles offer a dystopic chronology in two installments: in the first phase, indigenous criminal elements take over the small-town rural suburbs and in the second phase, nameless third world infidels housed in the UN make a final conquering manoeuver to rush the whole nation, making their first point of attack a leafy Michigan suburb. In this War of the Worlds, "we" (Sweeney's suburban militias) have to be prepared to liberate the nation. The first article goes by the title "Danger in the Safety Zone" in which the author notes parenthetically: "As violence spreads into small towns, many Americans barricade themselves" (Smolowe, 1993). In this article, murder and mayhem are everywhere outside the suburban home: in the McDonald's restaurant, in the shopping mall, in the health club, in the courtroom. The article also displayed statistics indicating that crime in the major cities had been declining somewhat while crime in the suburbs—the place where the middle classes thought there were safest—was now increasingly engulfing residents in random acts of violence. All of this is happening even in a place like "small town, U.S.A. , Tomball, Texas"—the most unlikely place for postmodernism's final confrontation with the other. The second article, "Patriot Games," is about the "mushrooming" of heavily armed white militia groups in training, preparing for the war of wars against the federal government and nameless, invading immigrants and political forces that the Clinton administration has somehow, unwittingly, encouraged to think that America is weak and lacking in resolve to police its borders:

> The members of the larger patriot movement are usually family men and women who feel strangled by the economy, abandoned by the government and have a distrust for those in power that goes well beyond that of the typical angry voter. Patriots join the militias out of fear and frustration. . . . [They] were particularly enraged when Congress passed a crime bill last August that banned assault weapons. . . . Patriots also fear that foreign powers, working through organizations like the United Nations and treaties like the General Agreement on Tariffs and Trade, are eroding the power of America as a sovereign nation. On a home video promoting patriot ideas, a man who gives his name only as Mark from Michigan says he fears that America will be subsumed into "one big, fuzzy, warm planet where nobody has any borders." Samuel Sherwood, head of the United States Militia Association in Blackfoot, Idaho, tells followers, absurdly, that the Clinton Administration is planning to import 100,000 Chinese policemen to take guns away from Americans. . . . When it comes to organization, however, the [militias] go high-tech. The militia movement, says Berlet, "is probably the first national movement organized and directed on the information highway." Patriot talk shows, such as *The Informed Citizen*, a half-hour program broadcast on public-access TV in Northern California, spread the word that American values are under attack from within and without. Militias also communicate via the Patriot Network, a system of linked computer bulletin boards, and through postings in news groups on the Internet. One recent posting by a group calling itself the Pennsylvania Militia, more specifically the F Company of the 9th Regiment, asked for a "few good men" to join up and "stand up to the forces of federal and world tyranny." (Farley, 1994, p, 48–49)

What does all of this mean? These articles, in some ways, announce a new sensibility and mood in the political and social life in the United States—a mood articulated in suburban fear of encirclement by difference—a mood increasingly formulated in a language and politics of what James and Nietzsche called "resentment." The dangerous inner city and the world "outside" are brought into suburban homes through television and film, releasing new energies of desire mixed with a fear of the images projected on the home entertainment screen.

As we are in the late '90s, increasingly, conflicts in education and popular culture are taking the form of grand panethnic battles over language, signs, and the occupation and territorialization of urban and suburban space. These conflicts intensify as the dual model of the city, of the rich and poor, dissolves into splintered and fragmentary communities signified by the roaming homeless on network television. For our late-twentieth-century Sweeney Erectus standing on the pyres of resentment in the culturally beleaguered suburbs, the signs and wonders are everywhere in the television evening news. Sweeney's cultural decline is registered in radically changing technologies and new sensibilities, in spatial and territorial destabilization and re-coordination, in the fear of falling, and in new, evermore incorrigible patterns of segregation and resegregation (Grossberg, 1992). Before his jaundiced eyes, immigrant labor, immigrant petty bourgeoisie now course through suburban and urban streets—the black and Latino underclasses after the Los Angeles riots, announces one irrepressibly gleeful news anchor—are restless. The white middle classes are experiencing declining fortunes, and the homeless are everywhere.

This new world order of mobile, marginal communities is deeply registered in popular culture and in social institutions such as schools. The terrain to be mapped here is what Hal Foster in the *Anti-Aesthetic* (1983) calls postmodernism's "other side"—the new centers of the simulation of difference that loop back and forth through the news media to the classroom, from film culture and popular music to the organization and deployment of affect in urban and suburban communities—Sweeney's homeground.

You will recall that Fredric Jameson (1984), in his now famous essay "Postmodernism, or the Cultural Logic of Late Capitalism," maintained that a whole new emotional ground tone separated life in contemporary post-industrial society from previous epochs. He described this emotional ground tone as "the waning of affect," the loss of feeling. While I agree with Jameson that emotions, like music, art, film, literature, and architecture, are historically determined and culturally bound, I disagree with his diagnosis that contemporary life is overwhelmingly marked by a certain exhaustion or waning of affect. I want to maintain that a very different logic is at work in contemporary life, particularly in

the area of race relations. Postmodernism's other side of race relations
... of the manipulation of difference ... is marked by a powerful
concentration of affect or the strategic use of emotion and moral re-
evaluation.

Central to these developments is the rise of the cultural politics of
"resentment." Nietzsche (1967), in *Genealogy of Morals*, defined resentment as the specific practice of defining one's identity through the
negation of the other. Some commentators on Nietzsche associate
resentment only with "slave morality." Here we are taken genealogi-
cally back to "literal slaves" in Greek society, who, being the most
downtrodden, had only one sure implement of defense: the acerbic use
of emotion and moral manipulation. I want to argue along with Robert
Solomon (see his "Nietzsche, Postmodernism and Resentment"), that
contemporary cultural politics are "virtually defined by bourgeois
resentment" (1990, p. 278). As Solomon maintains: "resentment elabo-
rates an ideology of combative complacency [or what Larry Grossberg
(1992) calls 'impassioned apathy']—a 'levelling' effect that declares society to be 'classless' even while maintaining powerful class structures and
differences" (p. 278). The middle class declares there are no classes
except itself, no ideology except its ideology, no party, no politics,
except the politics of the center, the politics of the middle, with a
vengeance.

A critical feature of discourses of resentment is their dependence on
processes of simulation. For instance, the suburban middle–class subject
knows its inner-city other through an imposed system of infinitely
repeatable substitutions and proxies: census tracts, crime statistics,
tabloid newspapers, and television programs, and lastly, through the
very ground of the displaced aggressions projected from suburban moral
panic itself (Beatty, 1994; Reed, 1992). Indeed, a central project of
PMC suburban agents of resentment is their aggressive attempt to hold
down the moral center, to occupy the center of public discourse, to
stack the public court of appeal. The needs of the suburbs therefore
become "the national interests" or what the Speaker of the House
might call the "legitimate demands of the hardworking American tax-
payers." By contrast, the needs of the inner city are dismissed as a waste-
ful "social agenda" of the out of center liberal left. Resentment is
therefore an emotion "distinguished, first of all, by its concern and
involvement with *power*" (Solomon, p. 278), and it is a power with its

own material and discursive logic. In this sense, it is to be distinguished from self-pity. If resentment has any desire at all, it is the "total annihilation ... of its target" (p. 279). Sweeney offers his own homemade version of the final solution: take the homeless and the welfare moms off general assistance; above all, build more prisons!

A new moral universe now rides the underbelly of the beast—late capitalism's global permutations, displacements, relocations, and reaccumulations. The effect has meant a material displacement of minority and dispossessed groups from the landscape of contemporary political and cultural life. That is to say, increasingly, the underclass or working-class subject is contemporaneously being placed on the outside of the arena of the public sphere as the middle-class subject-object of history moves in to occupy and appropriate the identity of the oppressed, the space of radical difference. The center becomes the margin. It is as if Primus Rex had decided to wear Touchstone's foolscap; Caliban exiled from the cave as Prospero digs in. Resentment operates through the processes of simulation that usurp contemporary experiences of the real, where the real is proven by its negation or its inverse. Resentment has infected the very structure of abstract value, and the battle over signs is being fought in cultural institutions across the length and breadth of this society. We are indeed in the midst of a culture war. We know this, of course, because avatars of the right like Patrick Buchanan (1992) and William Bennett (1994) constantly remind us of their books of values. As Buchanan put it bluntly, sometime ago, "The GOP Vote Search Should Bypass the Ghetto" (quoted in Omi and Winant, 1986, p. 124). From the cultural spiel of the 1992, 1994, and 1996 election campaigns—from family values to *Murphy Brown*, to the new corporate multicultural advertizing, from rap music, to the struggle over urban and suburban space, from the Rodney King beating, to Charles Stuart, to Susan Smith, to O. J. Simpson—a turf battle over symbolic and material territory is underway. The politics of resentment is on the way as the suburbs continue to draw resources and moral empathy away from the urban centers.

A fundamental issue, posed by Nietzsche and James, certainly an issue posed by their theories of identity formation, is the challenge of defining identity in ways other than through the strategy of negation of the other. This, I wish to suggest, is the fundamental challenge of multiculturalism, the challenge of "living in a world of difference" (Mercer,

1992). Education is indeed a critical site in which struggles over the organization and concentration of emotional and political investment and moral affiliation are taking place. This battle over signs (resentment) involves strategies of articulation and rearticulation of symbols in popular culture and the media. These signs and symbols are used in the making of identity and the definition of social and political projects. Within this framework, the traditional poles of left versus right and liberal versus conservative, Democrat versus Republican, are increasingly being displaced by a more dynamic and destabilizing model of mutation of affiliation and association. Another dimension of this dynamic is that the central issues that made the binary oppositions of race and class conflict intelligible and coherent in the past have now collapsed or have been recoded. The central issues of social and economic inequality that defined the line of social conflict between the left and the right during the civil rights period are now, in the post–civil rights era, inhabited by the new adversarial discourses of resentment. Oppositional discourses of identity, history and popular memory, nation, family, the deficit, and crime have displaced issues concerning equality and social justice. New Right publisher, William Rusher, articulates this displacement by pointing to a new model of material and ideological distinctions coming into being since the 1980s:

> A new economic division, pits the producers—businessmen, manufacturers, hard-hats, blue-collar workers, and farmers [middle America]— against a new and powerful class of non-producers comprised of the liberal verbalist elite (the dominant media, the major foundations and research institutions, the educational establishment, the federal and state bureaucracies) and a semipermanent welfare constituency, all coexisting happily in a state of mutually sustaining symbiosis. (Rusher quoted in Omi and Winant, 1986, p. 124)

Let us examine some manifestations of one of the principal articulations of resentment: the discourse of crime, violence, and suburban security. In the next section of this chapter, I will discuss examples from television evening news, film, and popular magazine and newspaper features that show the variability, ambiguity, and contradiction in this discourse of conflict. We will see that signifiers of the inner city as the harbinger of violence, danger, and chaos loop into the mass media and the suburbs and Hollywood and back again in the constructions of black male directors of the reality of the "hood" . . . then to the black male youth audience constructed as other to itself.

"REFLECTING REALITY" AND FEEDING RESENTMENT

Too often, Black artists focus on death and destruction arguing that it is what's out there so we got to show it! Please!! What needs to be shown is the diversity and complexity of African-American life

—*The Syracuse Constitution*, August 2, 1993, p. 5

The logic of resentment discourse does not proceed along a straight line in a communication system of encoding/decoding, nor does it work one-way from text to audience. Its tentacles are more defused, more rhizomatic and deeply intertextual. Resentment processes work from white to black and black to white, and white to Asian and Asian to white and so on, looping in and out and back again as second nature across the striated bodies of the inhabitants of the inner city—the black world available to the black director who delivers the black audience to Hollywood. The inner city is thereby reduced to an endless chain of recyclable signifiers that both allure and repel the suburban classes. The inner city is constantly prodded for signifiers of libidinal pleasure and danger.

But there is also the shared ground of discourses of the "authentic" inner city in which the languages of resentment and the reality of "the" hood commingle in films of black realism of black directors such as John Singleton and the Hughes brothers. It is a point that Joe Wood (1993) makes somewhat obliquely in his discussion of the film *Boyz 'N the Hood* (1992) which is set, incidentally, in South Central, Los Angeles. In an article published in the *Esquire* magazine entitled "John Singleton and the Impossible Greenback Bind of the Assimilated Black Artist," Wood notes the following:

> *Boyz*'s simplified quality is okay with much of America. It is certain that many whites, including Sony executives and those white critics who lauded the film deliriously, imagine black life in narrow ways. They don't want to wrestle with the true witness; it might be scarier than "hell." Sony Pictures' initial reaction to *Boyz* is instructive: John confides that the studio wanted him to cut out the scene in which the cops

harass the protagonist and his father. *"Why do we have to be so hard on the police?"* they asked. An answer came when Rodney King was beaten; the scene stayed in—it was suddenly "real." (August 1993, p. 64)

Here we see the elements of repeatability, the simulation of the familiar, and the prioritization of public common sense that television helps to both activate and stabilize. Hollywood drew intertextually on the reality code of television; television commodified and beautified the images of violence captured by a streetwise camera. Singleton's claim to authenticity, ironically, relied not on endogenous inner-city perceptions but, exogenously, on the overdetermined mirror of dominant televisual news. *Boyz 'N the Hood* could safely skim off the images of the inner city corroborated in television common sense. For these Hollywood executives, police brutality became real when the Rodney King beating became evening news. As Wood argues:

What Sony desired in *Boyz* was a film more akin to pornography . . . a safely voyeuristic film that delivered nothing that they did not already believe. . . . But how strenuously will they resist his showing how Beverley Hills residents profit from South Central gangbanging, how big a role TV plays in the South Central culture. . . (p. 65)

Of course, what even Joe Wood's critical article ignores about a film like *Boyz 'N the Hood* is its own errant nostalgia for a world in which blacks are centered and stand together against the forces of oppression—a world in which black men hold and practice a fully elaborated and undisputed paternity with respect to their children—a world that radically erases the fact that the location of the new realist black drama, Los Angeles, South Central, the memories of Watts, etc. , are now supplanted by an immigrant and a migrant presence where, in many instances, black people are outnumbered by Latinos and Asian Americans (Davis, 1992; Lieberman, 1992).

For instance, Latinos make up about 39 percent of the city's population and blacks make up 13 percent; Latinos slightly outnumber blacks in South Los Angeles (Lieberman, 1992). The Asian population is smaller than the black population; however, Asians are highly visible as small business entrepreneurs in the inner city. The complex racial ecology of the hood was apparent during the 1992 Los Angeles riots.

According to a RAND Corporation study of 5,633 adults arrested during the peak days of the riots, 51 percent were Latino, mostly young men aged eighteen to twenty-four. By contrast, only 36 percent of those arrested were black (Lieberman, 1992). Furthermore, approximately 40 percent of the businesses destroyed were owned by Latinos (Davis, 1992), although, Korean businesses were the most targeted, partly in revenge for the murder of fifteen-year-old Latasha Harlins by a Korean grocer, and partly as a signal to build more black-owned businesses in the predominantly black neighborhoods of South L.A.

Like the Hollywood film industry, the mainstream news media's address to black and brown America directs its gaze toward the suburban white middle class. It is the gaze of resentment in which aspect is separated from matter and substance undermined by the raid of the harsh surfaces and neon lights of inner-city life. In the sensation-dripping evening news programs of the networks—CBS, NBC, ABC, and CNN—as they pant and struggle to keep up with the inflamed journalism of the tabloids—black and Latino youth appear metonymically in the discourse of problems: "kids of violence," "kids of welfare moms," "car jackers," the "kids without fathers," "kids of illegal aliens," "kids who don't speak 'American.'" The skins of black youth are hunted down like so many furs. The inner city is sold as a commodity and as a fetish—a signifier of danger and the unknown that at the same time narrows the complexity of urban working-class life. You watch network evening news and you can predict when black and brown bodies will enter and when they will exit. The overwhelming metaphor of crime and violence saturates the dominant gaze on the inner city. For example, news coverage of the cocaine trade between the U.S. and Columbia routinely suggests that only poor and black inner-city residents use cocaine, not rich suburban whites who are actually the largest consumers of the illegal drug.

On any given day that Jesse Jackson might have given a speech on the need for worker solidarity, or Henry Cisneros on housing, or Congresswoman Maxine Walters on the budget, the news media are likely to pass over these events and show more sordid images of black crime and mayhem. This selection of images has become the reality of urban America. The inner-city's essence—empty but latent—combines paradigmatically with other images in the newspaper and film culture. It's an essence that has become a powerful crudescence: black bodies as semiotic cargo caught in the endless loop of the electronic media apparatus. The process is one of transubstantiation—so many black bodies ransacked for the luminous images of the subnormal, the bestial, "the crack kids," "the welfare brigade." The mass media's story of inner-city black and Latino people has less to do with an account about the denial of social services, poor public schools, chronic unemployment, the hacking to death of the public transportation system, the radical disinvestment in the cities, and the flight of jobs and resources to the suburbs—all of which can ultimately be linked to government neglect and deprioritization as middle-class issues of law and order, more jail space, and capital punishment usurp the Clinton administration's gaze on the inner city. Instead, the inner city exists as a problem in itself, and a problem to the world. The reality of the inner city is therefore not an endogenous discourse. It is an exogenous one. It is a discourse of resentment refracted back onto the inner city itself.

It is deeply ironic, then, that the images of the inner city presented by the current, new-wave black-cinema corroborate rather than critique mainstream mass media. Insisting on a kind of documentary accuracy and privileged access to the inner city, these directors construct a reality code of "being there" in the manner of gangster rappers. But black film directors have no *a priori* purchase on the inner city. These vendors of chic realism recycle a reality code already in the mass media. This reality code operates as a system of repeatability, the elimination of traces, the elaboration of a hierarchy of discourses—the fabrication and consolidation of specular common sense.

Menace II Society (1993), created by Allen and Albert Hughes, places the capstone on a genre that mythologizes and beautifies the violent elements of urban life while jettisoning complexities of gender, ethnicity, sexuality, age, and economy. Instead of being didactic, like *Boys 'N the Hood*, the film is nihilistic. The reality of the hood is built on a trestle of obviousnesses. Its central character, Caine Lawson (Tyrin Turner), is doomed to the drug-running, car stealing, meaningless violence that claim young men like himself (and before him, his father) from the time they can walk and talk. It is a world in which a trip to the neighborhood grocery can end in death and destruction. It is a world in which gangbangers demand and enforce respect at the point of a gun. This point is made at the very beginning of the movie when Caine and his trigger-happy buddy, O-Dog (Larenz Tate), feel disrespected by a

Korean store owner. The young men had come to the grocery to get a beer, but are provoked into a stand-off when the store owner hovers too close to them. The young men feel insulted because the Korean grocer makes it too obvious that he views them with suspicion. In the blink of an eye, O-Dog settles the score with a bout of unforgettable violence. When Caine and O-Dog leave, the store owner and his wife are dead. And, one act of violence simply precipitates another. By the end of the film, Caine, too, dies in a hail of bullets—payback by the gang of supporters of a young man that Caine had beaten up mercilessly earlier in the film.

This film sizzles with a special kind of surface realism. There is a lot of blood and gore in the hood in *Menace II Society*, and the camera-shot sequences consist, for the most part, of long takes of beatings or shootings. These shots are almost always extreme close-ups. Caine's life is supposed to be a character sketch of the inevitability of early death for inner-city male youth reared in a culture of violence; we have already seen it on the evening news before it hit the big screen. Black filmmakers therefore become pseudo-normative bards to a mass audience, who like the Greek chorus, already know the refrain. These are not problem-solving films. They are films of confirmation. The reality code, the code of the hood, the code of blackness, the code of Africanness, of hardness, has a normative social basis. It combines and recombines with suburban middle-class discourses such as the deficit and balancing the federal budget, taxes, overbearing, overreaching squandering government programs, welfare and quota queens, and the need for more prisons. It's a code drenched in public common sense. The gangster film has become paradigmatic for black filmic production out of Hollywood. And it is fascinating to see current films like Singleton's *Higher Learning* (1995) glibly redraw the spatial lines of the inner city and the suburbs in a campus town. *Higher Learning* is *Boys 'N the Hood* on campus. On the other hand, films like the Hughes brothers' most recent film *Dead Presidents* (1995) and Mario Van Peebles's *Panther* (1995) set the clock back, nostalgically, to the 1960s and the politics of the Vietnam War and black power—but the inner city remains, translucently, a place of historical ruin and degradation.

It is to be remembered that early in his career, before *Jungle Fever* (1991), Spike Lee was berated by mainstream white critics for not presenting the inner city realistically enough, for not showing the drug use and violence. Lee obliged with a vengeance in *Jungle Fever* in the harrowing scenes of the drug addict Vivian (Halle Berry) shooting it up at the "Taj Mahal" crack joint and the Good Doctor Reverend Purify (Ossie Davis) pumping a bullet into his son (Samuel Jackson) at point-blank range (Kroll, 1991).

By the time we get around to white produced films like *Grand Canyon* (1992) or *Falling Down* (1993), the discourse of crime, violence, and suburban security has come full circle to justify suburban revenge and resentment. In *Falling Down*, directed by Joel Schumaker, we now have a white suburban male victim who enters the hood to settle moral scores with anything and anyone that moves. Michael Douglas, as the angst-ridden protagonist, D-fens, is completely agnostic to the differences with and among indigenous and immigrant inner-city groups. They should all be exterminated as far he is concerned—along with, of course, his ex-wife who won't let him see his infant daughter. D-fens is the prosecuting agent of resentment. His reality code embraces Latinos who are gangbangers and Asian store owners who are portrayed as compulsively unscrupulous. In a scorching parody of gang culture, he becomes a one-man gang—a singular menace to society. In a calculated cinematic twist, the world of D-fens is characterized by a wider range of difference than the worlds depicted in black realist films. However, in this world, ironically, blacks are for the most part mysteriously absent from Los Angeles (Douglas feels more confident beating up on other racial groups). The question of the representation of the "real" inner city is, according to Aretha Franklin, "Who is zooming who?"

What is fascinating about a film like *Falling Down* is that it is also centered entirely around a single protagonist, a kind of proto-normative, anomic individual who, as James might put it, is "out there." He is the purveyor of what Jacques Lacan in his "mirror stage . . ." essay calls "paranoiac alienation" (Lacan, 1977, p. 5). Singlehandedly armed with more socio-normative fire power than any gangbanger could ever muster, D-fens is ready to explode as everyday provocations make him seethe to the boiling point. We learn, for instance, that he is a disgruntled, laid-off white collar employee—a former technician who worked for many years at a military plant. Displaced as a result of the changing economy of the new world order—displaced by the proliferation of different peoples who are now flooding Los Angeles in pursuit of the increasingly illusive American dream—D-fens is a semiotic prototype of a paranoid single white male who is frustrated by failure in the work-place and in personal relations with women. He is part of a growing anxiety class that blames government, immigrants, and welfare moms for its problems. A guy with a couple of chips on his shoulder and few hand-grenades to throw around, he is the kind of individual we are encouraged to believe a displaced middle-class person might become. As Joel Schumaker explains:

> It's the kind of story you see on the six o'clock news, about the nice guy who has worked at the post office for twenty years and then one day guns down his co-workers and kills his family. It's terrifying because there's the sense that someone in the human tribe went over the wall. It could happen to us. (Morgan, 1993)

D-fens is a kind of Rambo nerd who has seen too much computer software; a Perot disciple gone berserk. D-fens is spinning in the wheels of misfortune, caught in a sort of yup-draft. *Newsweek* magazine, that preternatural barometer of suburban intelligence, tells us that D-fens is the agent of a suburban resentment. D-fens's actions while not always defensible are "understandable":

> [The film] packs a pop-sociological punch. The fashionable revisionist reading of American history and culture that makes the white male the bad guy has triumphed, the film seems to argue, and it's made him not just defensive, but paranoid.... But *Falling Down*, whether it's really a mes-sage movie or just a cop film with trendy trimmings, pushes white men's buttons. The annoyances and menaces that drive D-fens bonkers— whining panhandlers, immigrant shopkeepers who don't trouble them-selves to speak good English, gun-toting gangbangers—are a cross-section of white-guy grievances. From the get-go, the film pits Douglas—the picture of obsolescent rectitude with his white shirt, tie, specs and astro-naut haircut—against a rainbow coalition of Angelenos. It's a cartoon vision of the beleaguered white male in multicultural America. This is a weird moment to be a white man. (Gates, March 29, 1993, p. 48)

D-fens's reactions are based on his own misfortunes and anger over dis-empowerment of the white middle class. Despite his similarities with the neo-Nazi, homophobic, army-surplus store owner in the movie, they are not the same type of social subject. Unlike the neo–Nazi, D-fens reacts to the injustices he perceives have been perpetrated against him. He is the post–civil rights scourge of affirmative action and reverse discrimination.

With *Falling Down*, Hollywood unleashes the final punctuation marks on a discursive system that is refracted from the mainstream electronic media and the press onto everyday life of the urban centers. Unlike D-fens in *Falling Down*, the central protagonist in *Menace II Society*, Caine, has nothing to live for, no redeeming values to vindicate. He is a preexistentialist—a man cut adrift in and by nature. What the film does share with *Falling Down* is a general subordination of the interests and desires of women and a pervasive sense that life in urban centers is self-made hell. Resentment has now traveled the whole way along a fully reversible signifying chain as black filmmakers make their long march along the royal road to a dubious Aristotelian mimesis in the declaration of a final truth. The reality of being black and inner city in America is sutured up in the popular culture. The inner city has no interior. It is a holy shrine to dead black and brown bodies—hyperreal carcasses on arbitrary display.

RESENTMENT EFFECTS

> *But the body is also directly involved in a political field; power relations have an immediate hold upon it; they invest it, mark it, train it, torture it, force it to carry out tasks, perform ceremonies, to emit signs.*
>
> —Michel Foucault, *Discipline and Punish*, 1979, 25

As the portrayals of the inner city in these films illustrate, the discourse of resentment not only has powerful rhetorical effects, it also has devastating material effects as well. Inner-city black school youth are surrounded by this powerful discourse of crime and violence in which they are the constructed other—social objects who grapple with the reality code projected from the popular media culture. Their experience of the reality code is grounded in material practices such as police harassment. Black and brown youth experience the reality code as a problem of representation. The reality code is translated in the discourse of resentment. Democracy asserts its tragic limits in the urban center. Unlike the cause-and-effect theories of the film culture, police harassment reported by high school students in the Los Angeles school system seems random and vicious.

A good example of the material consequences and challenges of representation for minority youth is provided in the stories told by inner-city adolescents at Liberty High School in Los Angeles. Liberty High is itself an extension of the long arm of the state. The L.A. Unified Public School system has its own police force. The following excerpt taken from an ethnographic study that I conducted in this inner-city high school about six months before the Rodney King beating gives a sense of the students' experiences with the unyieldingly negative representations of black and Latino male youth generated in the popular media. A switch point of this field of representation is their encounter with the police. This research was conducted in the summer of 1990. It involved an evaluation of Teach For America's Summer Institute preservice teacher internship program for its "corps members":

I report on a class that is taught by a Teach For America intern, Christopher Morrison. Christopher is a white male. He is about twenty-two years old at the time of the study. He hails from the South and has had some military training. His assignment to do a four-week teaching stint at Liberty High School is his first "exposure" to an inner-city school. Christopher's cooperating teacher is a black female, Ruby Marshall. She is in her sixties, anticipating retirement. Of the seventeen students that are in Christopher's classroom, fifteen are African American and two are Latino. The classroom discussion is taken over by students' accounts of police violence. Christopher introduces the topic of police harassment based on some queries made the previous day by one of his students, Rinaldo. But in the torrent of accounts offered by students, Christopher loses control of his class. So, too, does the cooperating teacher, Ruby Marshall. In effect the classroom has become a site for a therapeutic release—a show and tell on harassment and the "image problem" that black and brown male youth have with the Los Angeles police. Students detail acts of police harassment that have left them disoriented about their own senses of self and identity. One student reports that he had been stopped by the cops and searched for a gun; in his words, "The cops had no probable reason." Another reports that he was arbitrarily beaten up, in his view, for walking on the wrong street at the wrong time of night. One girl in the class tells of how she knew of friends whose houses, "was bust into." Many of them talked of intimidating stares and glares and threatening behavior on the part of the police.[2]

In this Los Angeles high school classroom, the diffusion of images of the police and the problematic relationship of some kids to the law opened up deep wounds of adolescent insecurity and identity crisis. Students were looking for solutions to problems about self-representation from their teachers who did not seem to have any easy answers. The students were concerned about how to represent themselves in ways that might help them to maintain their sense of adolescent freedom and individual rights and yet avoid the full-court press of the cops. The responses of the adults, Christopher Morrison and Ruby Marshall, were steeped in the common sense of the reality code—the code of mimesis; the code of resentment. Here are some of Ruby Marshall's comments on the students' reports of police harassment:

> I say if you walk like a duck and you hang out with ducks, then you are a duck. I believe that some of the things they [the police] do are not right. But you guys sometimes walk around without any books like the rest of the guys on the street. If you do that, they [the cops] will pull you over. . . . One day I saw them [some police officers]. They had this guy spread eagle against the car. And they were really harassing him. You should not hang out with these guys. . . . Don't hang out with the Bloods, or the Crips, or the Tigers!. . .When a group of you guys are hanging out together that gives them cause for concern. You don't even carry books. You need to be as non-threatening as possible.

To the latter remark, one student replied: "You mean to say that if I am going around with my friends at night I need to haul along a big old bunch of books over my shoulder?"

Some of the responses of the white student teacher, Christopher Morrison, conveyed a sense of ambivalence—great sympathy for the adolescent students as they reported examples of police harassment, but also a sense that the police had to go on "images," that they had to enforce the law, and that school youth had to exercise restraint and respect if they wished to be treated respectfully themselves. To the students' questions about free speech and freedom of movement, Christopher pointed them in the direction of the reality code where actions had real consequences; wrong was repaid by retributive sanctions, and personal errors of judgement—associating with the wrong crowd, and being in the wrong place at the wrong time—were actions that one had to accept responsibility for. Just as ordinary adult citizens had to accept the consequences for their actions, adolescents who challenge the law ought to be aware of the wrath of the law. Here follows an excerpt from a testy but revealing exchange between Christopher and his black students on the topic of the aggressive actions of the police: "Let me tell you a story about myself. Maybe this will help. Once I had some friends. They were hanging out on the college campus. But they did not look like college students. They were white, but they had long hair." A number of students interjected, "You mean like a hippie?" "Like a hippie," Christopher said. Then he continued with his story:

> They arrested these guys. You have to understand that the police go on images. They rely on images. They need categories to put people into so that they can do their work. And sometimes these categories are right. And if you, Morgan, had a gun [addressing the student who said the cops stopped and searched him for weapons] then you gave them probable cause. You fitted into one of their categories.

Morgan seemed utterly dismayed: "It wasn't the gun. They were just riding through the hood. If I had given them any trouble they would have sweated me." Christopher disagreed with this assessment of danger: "I don't think they would do that to you. You can complain if you feel that your rights have been abused. Look, people are being blown away at a faster rate than ever in this country. Just don't give them cause. If you got something [a gun] on you, then that is giving them cause."

On the matter of police harassment, the teachers, as representatives of the middle class, moved swiftly toward points of ideological closure. Their students, young and black and Latino and in trouble with the law, passed their adult mentors like ships in the night. They wanted the discourse opened up in ways that would allow their voices to be heard. But the Los Angeles classroom seemed more like a court of appeal in which the students appeared to lose the battle for control over their public identities and self-representation. The process of resentment had insinuated itself into the lives of the students. Black and Latino students had to contend with the burden of an always already existent complex of representations that constructs them as outsiders to the Law. The inner-city classroom, like the inner-city streets, in the language of

Thomas Dunn (1993), has become an "enclosure" for the containment of the mobility of black and brown youth. The border line between the suburbs and the traumatized inner city is drawn in public schools like Liberty High. And teachers like Ruby Marshall and Christopher Morrison stand guard on the frontlines—agents of resentment guarding the border zone erected around suburban interests.

CONCLUSION

With the politics of resentment now widely diffused, we have entered a new phase in race relations in education and society. These relations are propelled by the processes of simulation built into historically specific discourses such as crime, violence, and suburban security. It should be noted that both majority and minority groups use resentment discourses. Eurocentrism and Afrocentrism are two such discourses that thrive on the negation of the other. Proponents of these two world views attempt to reify moral centers, in opposition to supposed peripheries, not realizing that these moral centers are simulations of reality. In popular film and television culture, both of these discourses have been refracted onto the inner city with a vengeance. In this period of "the post" there are no innocent or originary identities (Bhabha, 1994).

With the politics of resentment, we are descending down the slippery slope of the war over signs. Traditional divisions and alliances no longer hold. As Baudrillard (1983) argues, opposition becomes only a hyper-simulation of opposition. Collusion of supposed extremes is the more common result. The battle lines over signs are now being drawn down in and around predictable constituencies, and whole new categories of association and affiliation enter the fray. The war over signs and symbols pits respectable suburban society against the amoral inner city—the nuclear-family residents of the sterilized suburban environments against the urban children without fathers. It pits supporters of academic freedom against the politically correct; a field of affect in which we see Marxists, such as Eugene Genovese, form a blood pact with slick proto-capitalist third world immigrant intellectuals like Dinesh D'Souza. Together, they harangue embattled indigenous first-world minorities. So much for the conservative wing of the travelling theorists.

Resentment is, therefore, negative and positive, decentering and recentering. While the inner city flounders under the weight of government disinvestment and the scarcity of jobs and services, old and new patriotic and fundamentalist groups led by Rambo, Ross Perot, the NRA, and Teach For America sing Rush Limbaugh's refrain: "We must take back America." Resentment themes may pit the organicists against the polluters or Bill Clinton, Rush Limbaugh, Tipper Gore, Dan Quayle, and the cops against the rappers. The battle over moral leadership, as Nietzsche once noted, is "drenched in blood" (1967, p. 133).

In a time of the fear of falling, the suburban middle-class subject stabilizes itself by dressing in the garb of "the oppressed"—people whose fortunes have been slipping despite their moral steadfastness. It is the middle class that feels increasingly surrounded by the other. Its public space overrun by the homeless. Its Toyotas and BMWs hijacked by the amoral underclass. And always, there is the question of what to do with urban youth who are out of control.

Those of us who are privileged, but in some ways, condemned to look at the world as perpetual voyeurs—Sweeneys of the sightless eyes warming in the glow of our ethereal hearths—cannot retreat forever from this tumultuous world of difference. We are part of a world of difference in which our needs and interests must be problematized and our sense of identity and community challenged. We must try to think within, but also think beyond, our immediate particularities. Those of us who articulate the anxieties repressed in and by our own privileged access to society's cornucopia of rewards—dwellers of the suburban city and the masters of the new fictive hyperrealisms of the hood—are responsible to the urban city which our practices of cultural production and over-consumption both create and displace.

NOTES

1.   Teach For America is the much talked about voluntaristic youth organization that has sought to make a "difference" in the educational experiences of disadvantaged innercity youth. The organization patterned on the can-do humanism of the Peace Corps, recruits graduates from elite universities and colleges around the country to serve a two-year stint in inner-city public schools districts desperate for teachers for schools that are severely understaffed.

2.   The cops also participate in their own language of gangbanging—keeping the peace with shiny guns and lots of leather. For instance, the stares

and glares of which the students complained are also minted and embossed on the Tupperware and bric-a-brac that you can find in *The Official Cop Catalog* (1992) of the Line Up Police Products Incorporated company, headquartered in San Luis Obispo, California—a sort of police-exclusive minimart in an emergent culture industry that circulates seductive and fascistic cop images back to the cops themselves. Like the producers of the gangster movies, the police are interested in authentic masculinity too. Hence, the 1992 Christmas *Official Cop Catalog* features "The Teddy Bear Line Up," of "Police Bear," "Mounty Bear," and "Fire Fighter Bear" for $54.95, $69.95, and $54.95 respectively. The ad tells its prospective audience that Police Bear "wears a shiny badge, an expert shooter's medal and even has embroidered patches. The bear's .357 [magnum] is worn in a holster, complete with thumb-break snap" (p. 1). On another page the catalog features a variety of mugs which portray various parodies of police daily work. On the back of a mug accompanying a picture of a police interrogation scene is the following disturbing message: "You walk in with a pretty face and information. You can't leave with both" (p. 24). Yet another mug depicts a "Hooker Lineup" of women before whom a chortling male cop asks his buddy "How much for the one on the right" (p. 25). Like Sam Spade, the police are both in the law and outside it. The displays on these mugs celebrate violence in which the police assert that as enforcers of the law, they are above it. These mugs celebrate various acts that appear to cross the line of lawful law enforcement and enter the zone of lawless perversity.

6

AFTER THE CONTENT DEBATE
Multicultural Education, Minority
Identities, Textbooks, and the
Challenge of Curriculum Reform

*Our country is a branch of European civilization. . . . "Eurocentricity" is
right, in American curricula and consciousness, because it accords with the
facts of our history, and we—and Europe are fortunate for that. The political
and moral legacy of Europe has made the most happy and admirable of
nations. Saying that may be indelicate, but it has the merit of being true and
the truth should be the core of any curriculum.*
—George Will, *Morning Advocate* December 18, 1989, p. 3

*Those who claim the superiority of Western culture are entitled to that claim
only when Western civilization is measured thoroughly against other civiliza-
tions and not found wanting, and when Western civilization owns up to its
own sources in the cultures that preceded it.*
—Toni Morrison, 1989, p. 2

While developments have taken place in contemporary popular culture
toward a certain radical eclecticism—a postmodern sensibility in the
areas of art, architecture, music, and literature, that in some ways
brazenly absorbs third world and ethnic images—the school system,
particularly the school curriculum, remains steadfastly monological. For
example, while popular artists such as David Byrne and Paul Simon
directly incorporate Afro-Brazilian and South African styles into their
music (albums such as *Rei Momo* and *Grace Land* are good examples),
and while minority artists like Spike Lee, Julie Dash, and the Afro-Asian
Black Arts movement in England have begun to influence new ethnic
themes in television and film culture, American educators have

responded with a decided lack of enthusiasm for cultural diversity and, at times, with a sense of moral panic with respect to the demands for a ventilation of the school curriculum (O'Connor, 1990). It is this administrative hostility to diversity that, over the years, has propelled minority agitation for multiculturalism in schooling.

Driven forward by demands from racially subordinated groups for fundamental reforms in race relations in education and society, and by the efforts of mainstream educators to provide practical solutions to the problem of racial inequality in the United States, multicultural education emerged in the late 1960s as a powerful challenge to the Eurocentric foundations of the American school curriculum (Pinar, Reynolds, Slatterly, and Taubman, 1995; McCarthy, 1995). Multiculturalism is a product of a particular historical conjuncture of relations among the state, contending racial minority/majority groups, educators, and policy intellectuals in the United States when the discourse over schools became increasingly racialized. From the first, African-Americans and other minority groups emphasized a variety of transformative themes, insisting that curriculum and education policy address the vital questions of the distribution of power and representation in schools and the status of minority cultural identities in curriculum organization and arrangements. (It should be understood in what follows that minority cultural identities are not fixed or monolithic but multivocal, and even contradictory. These identities are indeed "fluid" and are theorized here as the effects and consequences of the historically grounded experiences and practices of oppressed minority groups and the processes by which these practices and experiences come to be represented, reconstructed, and reinvented in daily life, in school, the workplace, the symbolic media, and in textbooks and curriculum. Minority identities are defined in the context of inter- and intra-group conflicts and in the context of encounters and struggles with dominant white groups.)

Within the last two decades, the transformative themes of the multicultural movement have been steadily "sucked back into the system" (Swartz, 1990). As departments of education, textbook publishers, and intellectual entrepreneurs pushed more normative themes of cultural understanding and sensitivity training, the actual implementation of an emancipatory multiculturalism in the school curriculum and in pedagogical and teacher education practices in the university has been effectively deferred. (Emancipatory multiculturalism is defined here as the critical redefinition of school knowledge from the heterogeneous perspectives and identities of racially disadvantaged groups—a process that goes beyond the language of "inclusivity" and emphasizes relationality and multivocality as the central intellectual forces in the production of knowledge.) Indeed, within the past few years, there has been a virulent reaffirmation of Eurocentrism and Western culture in debates over school curriculum and educational reform (Bloom, 1987; Hirsch, 1987; Ravitch, 1990; Herrnstein and Murray, 1994). The dominant curriculum exists as a powerful symbol of the contemporary American educator's willful retreat from the social and cultural heterogeneous communities surrounding the school in every urban center in this country.

In this chapter, I will situate the topic of multicultural education in the context of current debates over Eurocentrism and "Westernness" and the way these discourses are consolidated in the social studies textbooks used in American schools. I will conclude by offering some suggestions for curriculum and educational reform that can help to facilitate the project of an emancipatory multicultural education and the fostering of minority cultural identities in the classroom.

WESTERNNESS AND THE AMERICAN IDENTITY

Educators and textbook publishers have directly participated in the trotting out of a particularly cruel fantasy about the story of civilization and this society—one in which the only knowledge worth knowing and the only stories worth telling are associated with the handiworks of the bards of Greece and Rome. Within this frame of reference, art, architecture, music, and science, and democracy are portrayed as the fertile products of Europeans and their caucasian counterparts in the United States. It is, as Aime Cesaire (1983) would say, "a funny little tale to tell." This is, in fact, the essence of taught knowledge. Through the school curriculum and its centerpiece, the textbook, American schoolchildren come to know the world as one made by European ancestors and white people generally. The world that schoolchildren come to know is, on the other hand, a world over-populated by minorities and third world people, a world, according to Allan Bloom (1987), "brought to ruination," by these peoples of other lands. Contemporary conservative writers have sought to reinvigorate these myths. Bloom maintains in *The Closing of the American Mind* (1987) that it was the protests of African-American students and women in the 1960s that brought this country's university system and its curriculum to the present nadir. The reason why we are doing so poorly compared to the Japanese, others maintain, can be explained by the fact that we let the underprepared masses into the schools and the universities in the '60s (Herrnstein and Murray, 1994). Others, such as Diane Ravitch (1990), contend that though the American populace is diverse, the primary cultural and institutional coherence that currently exists in our society is unequivocally European in origin. It is the durability of these European values of order, democracy, and tolerance, Ravitch maintains, that has protected "us" from the cultural chaos afflicting countries in Eastern Europe, the Middle East, Africa, and Asia. ("The political and economic institutions of the United States were deeply influenced by European ideas. Europe's legacy to us is the set of moral and political values that we Americans subsequently refined and reshaped to enable us, in all our diversity, to live together in freedom and peace" [Ravitch, 1990, p. 20]).

But these kinds of remonstrations get us nowhere beyond nostalgia and its obverse, cynicism. Here we can find no real solace—no new ideas to help guide us through the events and challenges of the present era. This rather philistine reassertion of Eurocentrism and Westernness is itself a wish to run away from the task of coming to terms with the fundamental historical currents that have shaped this country—an impulse to deny the fundamentally, "plural," immigrant, and Afro-New World character that defines historical and current relations among minority/majority groups in the United States (Gates, 1992; Jordan, 1985, 1988).

To claim a pristine, unambiguous Westernness as the basis of curriculum organization as Bloom, E. D. Hirsh, Ravitch, and others suggest is to repress to the dimmest parts of the unconscious a fundamental anxiety concerning the question of African American and minority identities and "cultural presence" in what is distinctive about American life. The point I wish to make is one similar to the argument that Toni Morrison (1992) makes about Western literature in her brilliant book, *Playing in the Dark*: that is that, there is nothing intrinsically superior or even desirable about the list of cultural items and cultural figures celebrated by traditionalists like Hirsh and Bloom. It is to be remembered that at the end of the last century, the English cultural critic, Matthew Arnold, did not find it fit to include in "the best that has been thought and said" (Arnold, 1888, 1971; Czitrom, 1982) any existing American writer. This reminds us powerfully that what is "Western" is not synonymous with what is "American," no matter how hard some people may try. It also reminds us that the notion of Westernness is a powerful ideological construct—one thoroughly infused with an on-going social struggle over meaning and values (Bernal, 1987). What is Western is highly problematic as June Jordan (1985) has argued—do we want to claim that Ernest Hemingway is in and Toni Morrison is out? Where is the line of the Western to be drawn within school curriculum? Where does Westernness end and where does Americanness begin? No wonder that schools and universities have existed as hostile institutions with respect to the cultural identities of students of African-American, Asian, and Latino backgrounds. No wonder, then, that we are experiencing everywhere in this country what observers are calling a resurgence of racism and intolerance in educational institutions (Giroux, 1996). The school system still marginalizes minority youth with respect to access to instructional opportunity, access to an academic core curriculum, and so on. Our educational institutions are not genuinely multicultural or integrated even where those institutions are formally desegregated. Linda Grant (1984, 1985), in her ethnographic studies of desegregated schools, has shown that there is de facto segregation at these schools in terms of such variables as access to teacher time, and to the general material resources made available to minorities in the school setting. Grant (1984) argues that the organization of the curriculum at the desegregated school, concentrates African-American and Latino students in dead-end, non-academic tracks and contributes to minority failure, structurally facilitating the disorganization of minority identities by the processes of selection and labeling that designate these students as disproportionately "underachievers" and "at-risk."

The Textbook

Nowhere is this marginalization and suppression of minority cultural identities more in evidence than in the textbook industry in terms of the absence of minority history in school texts, and in terms of the exclusion of emancipatory indigenous scholarship in the process of textbook production altogether. But as I will argue, changes in the contents of textbooks are only one aspect of what is necessary for meaningful reform toward the goal of a genuine multicultural curriculum and school experiences for all students. There is, in fact, a need to look at a range of elements in the institutional culture of schools, the constraints and barriers to teacher ingenuity, and the educational priorities set in district offices, by building principals, and in teacher education programs in our universities. In all of these areas, emancipatory multiculturalism, as a form of what Henry Giroux (1985) and George Wood (1985) call critical literacy, is now suppressed.

Let us now consider the relationship of the textbook and the textbook industry to multicultural education. It is important to recognize from the outset that textbooks embody real, lived relations of representation, production, and consumption that tend more or less to suppress minority identities and reproduce existing social inequalities. By "representation," I am not simply referring to the presence or absence of pictures of minorities in textbooks. By representation, I mean the whole process of who gets to define whom, when, and how. Who has control over the production of pictures and images in this society? I believe that textbook production is an important dimension of a much broader social and political context in which minorities, women, and the physically and mentally disabled have little control over the process of the production of images about themselves. I mean, for example, that when incidents like the LAPD's beating of Rodney King occurs, black people do not have equal access to the media to tell their side of the story. So is it true in the case of textbooks.

In an essay entitled "Placing Women in History: Definitions and Challenges" (1975), the feminist historian Gerder Lerner, maintains that the treatment of women in contemporary textbooks can be described as presenting "compensatory" or "contribution" histories of the experiences of women in the United States. By compensatory history, Lerner refers to the tendency of dominant history textbooks to identify and single out what she calls "women worthies." This kind of history of notable women celebrates the achievements of individual women such as Jane Adams, Elizabeth Cady Stanton, Harriet Tubman, and so on, but compensatory history of this kind tends to marginalize the agency of the broad masses of minority and working-class women. As such, these compensatory textbooks, while more inclusive than earlier books, are not examplars of emancipatory or transformative scholarship.

This notion of compensatory history also applies to the treatment of minorities in textbooks. In the case of history, social studies, literature, and other discipline-based textbooks, minorities are added into an existing "order of things" (Foucault, 1970). One half of a page here and one half of a page there discusses slavery, Harriet Tubman, or "The Peaceful Warrior," Martin Luther King, Jr. There is no systematic reworking or restructuring of school knowledge, no attempt to present history from an alternative minority perspective. This fragmentary approach is also demonstrated in the treatment of the third world peoples of Africa, Latin America, and Asia. For instance, the editors of *Interracial Books for Children Bulletin* (1982), in an depth review of a "representative sample" of seventy-one social studies textbooks used in the '80s in American schools, report the following:

> Central America is entirely omitted from many of the most common world geography, history, and "cultures" textbooks used in U.S. classrooms. Thirty-one U.S. history texts were checked for their coverage of Central America. Seven of these do not even mention Central America. Fifteen texts limit coverage of Central America to the building of the Panama Canal, and most of these books ignore or mention only in passing the U.S. military intervention that led to the acquisition of the canal.... Not one of the thirty-one texts discusses the continuing involvement of the U.S. government—sometimes overt, sometimes covert—in Central America. (Editors, 1982, p. 12)

The U.S. imperial presence in Latin America is often narrated in a highly mythological discourse in which the United States emerges as the good Samaritan. The natives of South America cannot do without "our" help. U.S. paternalism is not only what the Latin Americans want, it is what is needed "down there" to keep hostile foreign powers from swallowing up the region and threatening "us":

> For a long time, the United States has been interested in Latin America. First, we have a large trade with our Latin-American neighbors. They send us products that we need and enjoy, such as tin, copper, coffee, bananas and chocolate. In turn, their people buy many products from the

United States. Second, the United States has tried to keep the Americas free from foreign control. If a strong and unfriendly nation controlled the nations near us, it would be a threat to the safety of the United States. (Schwartz and Connor, 1986)

This highly ethnocentric approach to history and social studies textbooks is stabilized by a language of universality and objectivity. In this way, the textbook is a central site for the preservation of a selective tradition in the school curriculum—one that pushes minorities and third world peoples to the outside, to the edge, to the point of deviance.

Perhaps the most pernicious feature of this dominant approach to school knowledge and textbook preparation is the tendency to avoid complexity and conflict. For example, in King and Anderson's *America: Past and Present* (1980), a fifth-grade social studies text used in Wisconsin's elementary schools, the only sustained discussion of the experiences of African Americans is in the context of slavery. Here, the treatment of slavery as a topic is done in a perfunctory manner, and the relations between whites and blacks on the slave plantation is described in benign terms, free of the symbolic and physical violence that characterized the slaves' daily existence. Complete with supporting illustrations of life on the plantation that make the slave plantation look like a California vineyard with the slaves living comfortably and snugly in their cabins, *America: Past and Present* describes life on the plantation in the following terms:

> On any plantation you visited in the South you would find that all of the farm workers were black slaves. Southern plantations came to depend on slavery. By 1750 there were more slaves than free people in South Carolina. On the plantation you visit, the slaves live in cabins near the fields. Since the slaves get no money for their work, they depend on their owners for clothes and food. The food is mostly salt pork and corn. Some of the slaves have tiny plots of land where they can grow vegetables. (King and Anderson, 1980, pp. 149–50).

It is interesting to compare this description with the writings on the slave plantation of indigenous authors such as Vincent Harding in his, *There Is a River* (1983), or C.L.R. James in *The Black Jacobins* (1963). In his discussion of slavery in Haiti, James draws on this eyewitness account:

A Swiss traveller has left a famous description of a gang of slaves at work. "They were about a hundred men and women of different ages, all occupied in digging ditches in a cane-field, the majority of them naked or covered with rags. The sun shone down with full force on their heads. . . . A mournful silence reigned. Exhaustion was stamped on every face, but the hour of rest had not yet come. The pitiless eye of the Manager patrolled the gang and several foremen armed with long whips moved periodically between them, giving stinging blows to all who, worn out by fatigue, were compelled to take a rest—men or women, young or old." This was no isolated picture. The sugar plantations demanded an exacting and ceaseless labour. (James, 1963, p. 10)

In *There Is a River,* Harding draws attention to another dimension of plantation life given short shrift in history textbooks used in our schools: the topic of black liberation struggles. He makes the following contention about the impact of liberation struggles on the planter-mercantile class in colonial America:

But it was not in Virginia and South Carolina alone, not only among white Southern society, that the fear of a black quest for freedom existed; the same attitude permeated much of Northern colonial life. In the Northern colonies blacks had already given evidence of their struggle for freedom. As early as 1657 Africans and Indians in Hartford "joined in an uprising and destroyed some buildings" in the settlement. Such incidents were regularly repeated. (Harding, 1983, p. 31)

In sharp contrast to the works of Harding and James, the bland, non-conflictual writing that one finds in many textbooks is in part a product of the highly routine, unchanging approach to textbook production conducted in the textbook industry. As publishers work to maximize markets and profits, textbook writing has become increasingly more and more like an assembly-line process in which multiple authors produce submissions that are checked for quality control, readability, and overly controversial content issues by keen editorial staffs (Apple, 1993). When the textbook finally becomes a finished product, we have a tool for teaching that is often uninteresting and unchallenging to students and teachers alike. By bargaining away issues that might offend state adoption committees and conservative interest groups, publishers, and textbook writers contribute to the marginalization of cultural diversity and the suppression of minority history and identities in textbooks.

Multicultural Reform

As indicated previously in this text, we must see the textbook as only one aspect of a broad set of practices that impact on the institutional environment of the school. School critics and government officials are now talking about curriculum reform without recognizing the pivotal role of the classroom teacher. Curriculum reform proposals such as "critical thinking," "scientific literacy," and "problem solving in mathematics," are coming from the outside, from researchers, politicians, and the business sector to teachers as slogans, in some cases, already packaged and teacher-proof (Apple, 1996). No matter how well-meaning many of these new proposals are, we run a very real risk of precipitating a loss of teacher autonomy in the classroom.

Mobilization for multicultural education reform must follow a very different path. Initiatives in this area must be situated in the context of broad structural and organizational reform in schooling. In most urban centers in this country, teachers presently work in school settings in which:

(a) They are underpaid (McCarthy, 1990, 1995).

(b) The principal, except in a number of exemplary circumstances, is subject to enormous administrative demands that impact on his/her effectiveness as an instructional leader. Excessive administrative demands directly limit the building principal's involvement in instructional improvement—whether these demands relate to critical thinking, or multiculturalism, or some other curriculum reform (McCarthy and Schrag, 1990).

(c) There is considerable institutional isolation. Teachers complain of not having the time to meet and plan, and that such collaboration is not explicitly encouraged or materially supported (McCarthy, 1990). Consequently, there is little peer supervision or collegiality as a result.

(d) Despite the rhetoric of "restructuring," school district offices are driven by a narrow sense of excellence, accountability, and educational achievement. Critical issues such as the need for multicultural reform in education are not given priority status (McCarthy and Schrag, 1990).

Of course, it is important to recognize, as Steven Purkey and Robert Rutter (1987) argue, that not all urban schools are beset by these barriers to critical teaching and learning. Some schools do have dynamic and progressive learning environments in which teachers pursue critical and emancipatory goals (Bastian, Fruchter, Gittell, Greer, and Haskins, 1986; Apple, 1996). But in a general sense, it can be said that teachers and educators in urban centers have been presented with a crisis of legitimacy with respect to the project of multicultural reform. In a society where the government has clearly reneged on its promise of racial equality, made during the Johnson and Kennedy administrations in the '60s, teachers and educators are being bombarded with new and contradictory demands. They are being asked to generate an ethos of harmony and equality at the same time that they are having to respond to increasing governmental pressure to foster competitive individualism in schools. This emphasis on competition is reflected in the dominant role of standardized testing in pedagogical practices, and the narrow range of classroom knowledge that is actually taught in the urban setting. Teachers feel compelled to be conservative about what they teach, and multiculturalism in this context is regarded as something of a supplement to a school curriculum that is oriented toward "the basics."

In other ways, too, federal policy within the last decade and a half of cutting back on financial support for the education and the overall social welfare of low-income students has sent out a message that has been destructive for the education of minorities. The message is this: TO HELL WITH EQUALITY. WE WANT TO COMPETE WITH THE JAPANESE. In a period when resources are becoming scarce, the gap between winners and losers is widening. Black and Hispanic youth have fallen victim to a system that says: YOU ARE NOT A PRIORITY. . . . YOU DO NOT REALLY MATTER. These developments are part of the bitter legacy of the Reagan era, but in many respects, the current administration in Washington has not offered any respite from the pattern of disinvestment in the urban centers that was initiated by Richard Nixon and Ronald Reagan.

Ironically, all of this is occurring at the same time as school populations are becoming more ethnically diverse. In the country's largest school systems, the majority of students are now minorities (*Education Week*, May 14, 1986; Hacker, 1995). Indeed, current demographic projections indicate that by the third decade of the twenty-first century, a third of the American population will be minority. These demographic changes raise profound questions about school knowledge; particularly, the wisdom of maintaining the rather unventilated dominance of the Eurocentric curriculum in our educational institutions. The Eurocentric curriculum is, in a manner of speaking, being overtaken by events. These developments should not lead to paralysis, but to action for comprehensive reform in schooling. Multicultural proponents should not focus merely on curriculum content, but should also introduce broader brush strokes of educational reform that would promote structural reorganization in schooling. Such structural reorganization should involve as a first priority the restoration of the professional space of the teacher as well as the full integration and the guarantee of equality of access to instructional opportunity for minority and underprivileged children. For the multicultural curriculum to be fully realized in schools, the following specific initiatives are absolutely critical:

(1) Preservice teacher education programs at the universities and colleges across the country must systematically incorporate critical multicultural objectives into their curricula and field experiences.

(2) School districts and school principals must set diversity as an explicit goal and seek ways to integrate the notion in the organization of the curriculum and the institutional life of schools. Right now, multiculturalism is treated as a side topic, mentioned only during Black History Month and on International Women's Day.

(3) Multiculturalism should not be limited to the present understanding—that is, the idea that all we need to do is to add some content about minorities and women to the school curriculum. Multiculturalism must involve a radical rethinking of the nature of school knowledge as knowledge that is fundamentally relational and heterogeneous in character. In this sense, for example, we cannot get a full understanding of the civil rights movement in the United States without studying its multiplier effects on the expansion of democratic practices to excluded groups in Australia, the Caribbean, Africa, England, and the United States itself. Further, we cannot properly

understand the development of European societies without an understanding of the direct link between Europe's development and the underdevelopment of the third world. For example, at the time that the French were helping to bankroll the American Revolution, two-thirds of France's export earnings were coming from its exploitation of sugar cane plantations in Haiti (James, 1963).

(4) Such a reworking of school knowledge must go a step further toward a reconsideration of the privileging of Eurocentric perspectives and points of view in the curriculum as reflected in, for example, the "famous men" approach to history. The "new" multicultural curriculum must go beyond the "language of inclusion" toward a "language of critique" (Giroux, 1985, 1996). This would involve the affirmation of minority identities and perspectives as the organizing principles for school knowledge. In this manner, schools would be sites for multicultural curriculum reform and pedagogical practices that are truly liberatory.

(5) Schoolteachers must be centrally involved in the reworking of the curriculum and the reorganization of the school in ways that give them a sense of professional autonomy and ownership over curriculum changes.

(6) There is a tremendous need to revise the K–12 exam system in this country which now places an overwhelming emphasis on standardized, multiple choice, and short answer tests. Also, it is absolutely critical that these exams begin to reflect the emphasis on multiculturalism that I have argued for in this chapter. At present, there is little incentive for teachers to teach and for students to learn more about minorities and women if these topics are not reflected in testing.

(7) In terms of textbooks, there is a need to involve indigenous minority and third world scholars and teachers in the production of school knowledge in the textbook industry at every level—that is, from the level of textbook writing, through editorial and managerial decision making.

(8) Lastly, let me return to a theme that I stressed at the beginning of this chapter: THE MULTICULTURAL ETHOS IN SCHOOLS WILL ONLY BE FULLY REALIZED WHEN MINORITY AND UNDERPRIVILEGED STUDENTS HAVE ACCESS TO AN ACADEMIC CORE CURRICULUM THAT IS ON PAR WITH THEIR MIDDLE–CLASS AND WHITE COUNTERPARTS.

Multicultural curriculum reform must mean that we seriously consider all of these elements. It should not mean simply incremental changes in curriculum content, but should involve wider educational, pedagogical, and curriculum reforms. These reforms should encourage the participation of indigenous scholars and classroom teachers in the production of school knowledge rooted to minority cultural identities, and facilitate the equal access to an academic core curriculum (that is critical as well as multicultural), for minority and underprivileged youth now significantly excluded from these crucial educational experiences.

CONCLUSION

In this chapter, I have sought to call attention to the urgent need to rethink the current privileging of Eurocentric ideas in our contemporary American school curriculum. I believe that this Eurocentric emphasis is misplaced in the light of the rapid diversification now taking place in school populations all across the United States. A fundamental place to start rethinking is the school textbook and the process of textbook production on the whole. Nevertheless, this is not enough to insure that our students will have a genuinely emancipatory multicultural experience in schooling. As I have maintained, multiculturalism must involve a wider range of educational change that would address the professional needs of the classroom teacher and the burning issue of equality of access for minorities to an academic curriculum. The needs of teachers and minority students must be understood as critical organizing principles in the movement toward multicultural curriculum reform as we go into the twenty-first century.

7

THE LAST RATIONAL MEN
Citizenship, Morality, and the Pursuit of Human Perfection

(with Ed Buendia, Heriberto Godina, Shuaib Meacham, Carol Mills,
Maria Seferian, Theresa Souchet, and Carrie Wilson-Brown)

> First Citizen: *We are accounted poor citizens, the patricians good.*
> *What authority surfeits on would relieve us. If they*
> *would yield us but the superfluity while it were*
> *wholesome, we might guess they relieved us humanely;*
> *but they think we are too dear; the leanness that*
> *afflict us, the object of our misery, is as an*
> *inventory to particularize their abundance; our*
> *sufferance is a gain to them. Let us revenge this with*
> *our pikes ere we become rakes. For the gods know I*
> *speak this in hunger for bread, not in thirst for revenge.*
>
> —*Coriolanus*, Act I, Scene I, lines 15–25,
> in Barnett, 1972, p. 1324

The opening speeches in William Shakespeare's play, *Coriolanus*, launch its characters and their audience into a debate among Roman plebeians about the status and quality of societal membership offered to the lower classes in Rome. This discussion is not simply about the conditions of the people in ancient Rome; Shakespeare was addressing the issue of citizenship in seventeenth-century England. This discussion of citizenship echoes forward into contemporary debates over identity and nation in the United States, in which Richard Herrnstein and Charles Murray's *The Bell Curve* (1994) represents just one strand of a larger network of discourses aiming at legitimizing and naturalizing a "white popular wisdom" (Murray, 1984), particularly regarding the inhabitants of the depressed urban centers. Taken as a whole, Herrnstein and Murray's volume is an especially disturbing register of contemporary anxiety over the boundaries of national affiliation and citizenship.

Herrnstein and Murray's book is a project of social normalization par excellence. Their objective is to call attention to the variable distribution of human mental capacity and moral virtue in American society and the implications that these "variables" have for the overall productivity and economic efficiency of the nation. As in Shakespeare's *Coriolanus*, there is a powerful deployment of tropes linking biology to morality and citizenship in *The Bell Curve*. For these two neoconservative social scientists, high IQ social actors are likely to be good citizens, low IQ types are likely to be bad. A clear policy implication flows from this formulation, society must find a way to limit and contain the reproduction of its flawed members. In this chapter, *The Bell Curve* will be considered as an example of the popular medical panic prose genre (see for e.g. the film *Outbreak* [1995] or Richard Preston's *The Hotzone* [1994] or Laurie Garrett's *The Coming Plague* [1994], all of which deal with the threat of invasion of exotic viruses and microbes into pristine American metropolitan suburbs) and its biological treatment of the topic of citizenship. Our primary focus in this essay will be chapter 12, and other related chapters of Herrnstein and Murray's book that address the topic of citizenship.

In *Coriolanus*, the plebeians speak for the alienated working classes of all times and all places. They denounce the arrogance and ill-gotten gains of society's patrician elites. But most importantly, they call attention to the obligations of society's rich to its poor and downtrodden and the obligations of state elites to the lower classes whose surplus value these elites rip off:

> *Menenius:* I tell you, friends, most charitable care
>   Have the patricians of you. . .
> *First Citizen:* Care for us! True, indeed! They ne'er cared for us
>   yet. Suffer us to famish, and their storehouses
>   crammed with grain; make edicts for usury, to
>   support usurers; repeal daily any wholesome act
>   established against the rich, and provide more
>   piercing statutes daily to chain up and restrain
>   the poor.
>   —*Coriolanus*, Act I, Scene I, lines 66–67, 80–87,
>   in Barnett, 1972, p. 1325)

Shakespeare gives the plebeian working classes a voice in *Coriolanus*. In *The Bell Curve*, Herrnstein and Murray take the voice of the poor away. Instead, society's downtrodden are the objects of an imperial biological gaze. In the minds of these authors, the poor exist to be defined, categorized and regulated. Whereas the plebeians in *Coriolanus* maintain that the issue of inequality is central to any discussion of citizenship, Herrnstein and Murray radically shove the issue of social inequity aside. For these authors, modern American society already offers equality of opportunity to all its citizens. The fact that some individuals and groups do not fare well in this open and freely competitive system has to do with their genes not their socioeconomic circumstances ("Low IQ continues to be a much stronger precursor of poverty than the socioeconomic circumstances in which people grew up," p. 127). *And, no policy intervention will change that fact.*

The Bell Curve, then, is an example of theorizing from the top of the food chain. Herrnstein and Murray take advantage of the panic already constructed by neo-nationalist movements: the Cultural Literacy movement (Hirsch, 1987; Bloom, 1987), the Anti-Immigration movement, and jingoistic isolationist groups such as patriot militias. They elaborate a proto-fascist defense of the existing system of unequal membership status offered to the working class and racially oppressed groups of America's citizenry. The authors pursue this objective of political inoculation of the hegemonic social order by using the discourse of biology to throw up a blanket of ideological protection around America's professional middle-class and corporate elites. Instead, Herrnstein and Murray point an accusatory finger at the country's minority and white working-class poor who, for the most part, they contemptuously dismiss as mentally degenerate. They are economically poor, the authors charge, because they are poor in cognitive capital. Instead of addressing the issue of the rights of society's most disadvantaged citizens and the obligations of the state, their focus is on the issue of moral responsibility and civic duty, and society's need for the most efficient deployment of the mental capacities of its citizenry. The view from Herrnstein and Murray's window on the world is decidedly corporatist. Given this emphasis, the authors write off the lower classes as the tragic ballast weighing down the ship of the state.

Interestingly, in Shakespeare's *Coriolanus*, it is Menenius, the apologist for Rome's patrician elite, who, like Herrnstein and Murray, uses poignant biological tropes in his ideological rationalization of the inequality in Rome's social order:

> *Menenius*: There was a time when all the body's members
>   Rebelled against the belly; thus accused it;
>   That only like a gulf it did remain
>   I' th' midst o' th' body, idle and unactive,
>   Still cupboarding the viand, never bearing
>   Like labor with the rest; where th' other instruments
>   Did see and hear, devise, instruct, walk, feel,
>   And, mutually participate, did minister
>   Unto the appetite and affection common
>   Of the whole body. The belly answered—
> *First Citizen*: Well, sir, what answer made the belly? . . .
> *Menenius*: Note me this good friend
>   Your most grave belly was deliberate,
>   Not rash like his accusers, and thus answered:
>   "True it is my incorporate friends," quoth he,
>   "That I receive the general food at first,
>   Which you do live upon; and fit it is,
>   Because I am the storehouse and the shop
>   Of the whole body. But, if you do remember,
>   I send it through the rivers of your blood,
>   Even to the court, the heart, to th' seat o' th' brain;
>   And, through the cranks and offices of man,
>   The strongest nerves and small inferior veins
>   From me receive that natural competency
>   Whereby they live; and though that all at once"—
>   You, my good friends, this says the belly, mark me. . .
> *First Citizen*: It was an answer. How apply you this?
> *Menenius*: The senators of Rome are this good belly.
>   And you, the mutinous members.
> —*Coriolanus*, Act I Scene I, lines 97–107, 129–142, 149–151,
>   in Barnett, 1972, pp. 1325–1326

Herrnstein and Murray's use of biological metaphors draws on a long tradition in the educational and social sciences. The use of medical or biological imagery to interpolate society runs deep in sociological and educational literatures; from the writing of Herbert Spencer to Edward Thorndike to Talcott Parsons and contemporary structural functionalist curriculum theorists such as Allan Ornstein and Francis Hunkins. This mainstream social science research tradition generally compares society to an organism. Much attention is paid to social norms and social normalization and the role of social institutions in the reproduction and maintenance of a functional equilibrium within the body politic. Similarly, behavioral scientists in the field of psychology have concentrated relentless attention on the measurement of human traits as already given in nature. This, for example, allows for the discursive production of glib taxonomies and systems of classification of individuals and groups into hierarchical categories of competence and efficiency. Early behavioral psychologists such as H. H. Goddard, Lewis Terman, and B. F. Skinner promised a world of human perfection through the unyielding practices of diagnosing and eliminating human decrepitude. In *The Bell Curve*, Herrnstein and Murray think they have found a pathway to this promised land. Access to the promised land lies in the harnessing and efficient deployment of human intelligence.

In their approach to the assessment of human intelligence and its function in organizing society, Herrnstein and Murray place their work within the most conservative behavioral science tradition, psychology— a tradition that runs through the genealogical line of Charles Spearman, Lewis Terman, Arthur Jensen, and William Schockley to contemporary thinkers such as Phillipe Rushton. This conservative or "classical" approach to cognition maintains that intelligence is massively heritable, and that the underlying causal explanation of virtually every social ill— unemployment, poverty, crime, illegitimacy, divorce and so on—is a matter of impoverished genetic endowment.

In *The Bell Curve*, Herrnstein and Murray deploy a tautological net of biological discourses in their analysis of the relationship of intelligence to citizenship. These discourses are used in three interrelated ways: biological tropes underscore the authors' claims of scientific neutrality; biological tropes help to draw out the lines of demarcation that separate the mentally degenerate working class from the mentally whole in the suburbs; and lastly, the language of biology is used to displace and suppress more radical discourses of social inequality. Let us take a closer look at the deployment of biological discourses in Herrnstein and Murray's book.

THE CLOAK OF SCIENTIFIC NEUTRALITY

These authors of *The Bell Curve* use the discourses of biology and nature to wrap their highly motivated and socially prejudicial claims in the cloak of scientific neutrality. The language of genes and heredity suggests a world in which "the social" literally evaporates and the contents and capabilities of "men's minds" are all that matter. Herrnstein and Murray try on their lab coats and wear them into the murkiest of waters in their assault on the poor:

> Going on welfare really is a dumb idea, and that is why women who are low in cognitive ability end up there, but also such women have little to take to the job market, and welfare is one of their few appropriate recourses when they have a baby to care for and no husband to help. (p. 201)

Here the discourse of measured intelligence, provides a cloak for a highly loaded moral didacticism and a deep suspicion of the autonomy and civic judgement of the nation's female poor. Poor, low IQ women do not make good citizens because they do not pull their weight. In addition, they endanger the economic (and the military) security of the nation by their hyper-fertility. This is just a fact of biology, not politics or ideology, Herrnstein and Murray argue. By emphasizing the scientificity of their work, Herrnstein and Murray portray themselves as expert citizens—professionals who are direct and honest with the rest of society; even if, by so doing, it means that they anger liberals and radicals and damn the lives of generations of various racial groups and the poor. This use of the discourse of biology invokes "science" abstractly and generally. Ultimately, the discourse of biology and nature constitutes a language of innocence—a discourse of the future linked to the past. In this recourse to nostalgia, the scientist and the citizen are one: dwellers of suburbia where the pursuit of the good life is the social reward for the best and brightest.

METAPHORS OF HUMAN PERFECTION

The second use of the discourse of biology foregrounds metaphors of perfection and their opposite, metaphors of human degeneracy. This deployment of biology represents the professional middle-class (PMC) persona as the human ideal, high in the mystical "g"—a complete and separate human specimen, distinct and distinguishable from the low cognitive dweller of the inner city. The professional middle-class subject is therefore the natural recipient of the genetic bounty of high cognitive capacity. And from this great bountiful storehouse, this PMC citizen dispenses "civility" and magnanimity to all his neighbors. He is the grand role model, the embodiment of the best and the brightest in civil society:

> Much of what could go under the heading of civility is not readily quantified. Mowing the lawn in the summer or keeping the sidewalks shoveled in the winter, maintaining a tolerable level of personal hygiene and grooming, returning a lost wallet, or visiting a sick friend... [This is] what we are calling civility. (p. 254)

As a corollary to this, suburban life is represented as the epitome of wholesomeness and completeness. The suburb is the incubator of civility—an organic environment in which the high IQ citizen helps his neighbor out, has open-ended, urbane conversations around the picnic table about politics and enters the voting booth, society's "civic hearth" (p. 255), to do his civic duty. This application of the discourse of biology is linked to a discourse of the natural habitat where the PMC citizen resides. Here, also, the discourse of nature blends with the discourse of nostalgia:

> We do not need statistics to remind Americans alive in the 1990s of times when they felt secure walking late at night, alone, even in poor neighborhoods and even in the largest cities. (p. 236)

What Herrnstein and Murray designate as "citizenship," the middle-class suburban resident already possesses as symbolic capital. This is summarized in the metaphors of self-regulation and self-control:

> To what extent is high intelligence associated with the behaviors associated with "middle-class values"? The answer is that the brighter young people . . . are also the ones whose lives most resemble a sometimes disdained stereotype. They stick with school, are plugging away in the workforce, and are loyal to their spouse. In so far as intelligence helps

lead people to behave in these ways, it is also a force for maintaining a civil society. (p. 236)

In subtle, and not so subtle, ways, Herrnstein and Murray center the polity in the suburb. Outside the acropolis dwells society's problem species: "the dull" and "the very dull," mostly urban inhabitants—Franz Fanon's "wretched of the earth" (1965). The body politic of the suburban high IQ citizen is healthy and wholesome. By contrast, the imagery associated with the low IQ poor is that of disease and degradation. If the problems of the urban centers are intractable or "chronic," as Herrnstein and Murray maintain, it has to do with the people who live there—the low IQ types who wallow in a culture of poverty:

> The analyses provide some support for those who argue that a culture of poverty tends to transmit chronic welfare dependency from one generation to the next. But if a culture of poverty is at work, it seems to have influence primarily among women who are of low intelligence (p. 191).

This culture of poverty is definitively linked to mental frailty. In a striking way, too, such poverty is decidedly gendered. The low IQ woman of America's working classes makes for a poor citizen because she lacks those values of self-regulation and self-control associated with the middle class. Here again the sense of disease and degeneracy is in the air:

> The disquieting finding is that the worst environments for raising children, of the kind that not even the most resilient children can easily overcome, are concentrated in the homes in which the mothers are at the low end of the intelligence distribution. (pp. 203–4)

Herrnstein and Murray draw down the lines between desired citizen traits and behaviors and undesirable ones by pointing to the almost indelible behavioral differences that exist between the woman of "middle-class values" and the "other" woman—the female urban resident who is bereft of these desirable middle-class traits and qualities:

> A woman in the NLSY [National Longitudinal Study of Youth] got a "Yes" if she had obtained a high school degree, had never given birth to

a baby out of wedlock, had not been interviewed in jail, and was still married to her first husband. People who failed any one of the conditions were scored "No." Never-married people who met all other conditions except the marital one were excluded from analysis. (p. 263)

In foregrounding issues of biology, reproduction and sexuality (that is, issues of control over the body), the authors of *The Bell Curve* separate out the inner-city dweller as an anti-citizen, a threat to the future security of the nation as a whole. The authors hint at these dangers throughout chapter twelve. They spell out the nature of this threat more definitively, however, in chapter fifteen which deals with present and future population and demographic trends. The matter can be summarized as follows. While the patriotic high IQ suburban resident is a model of restraint, the low IQ population of the country is aggressively fertile. Thus overall intelligence in the nation is declining because the very dull are producing too many babies, and the very bright too few. Worst yet, immigration policies are too generous to low-IQ immigrants from the third world. The result is the powerful negative phenomenon of overall decline in intelligence or "dysgenesis":

Mounting evidence indicates that demographic trends are exerting downward pressure on the distribution of cognitive ability in the United States and that the pressures are strong enough to have social consequences. . . . The professional consensus is that the United States has experienced dysgenic pressures throughout the century. . . . Women of all races and ethnic groups follow this pattern in similar fashion. There is some evidence that blacks and Latinos are experiencing even more severe dysgenic pressures than whites, which could lead to further divergence between whites and other groups in future generations. (p. 341)

BIOLOGY AND THE REPRESSION OF THE POLITICAL

The third type of deployment of biological metaphors in *The Bell Curve* involves a strategy of suppression of the discourse of the social and the political and their replacement by the discourse of nature. Here, the issue of inequality is displaced from the arena of the economy onto the terrain of mental and moral capacity and adequacy. The social world is naturalized as a world of the survival of the fittest. The best and the brightest of society's citizenry will prevail over the feebleminded. This is nature's law: social Darwinism writ large. Most significantly, Herrnstein and Murray suggest that the socioeconomic class map of America is obsolete, since Americans generally now all co-exist on a level playing field for contest mobility. They replace the class map of America with a cognitive map based on the distribution of mental capital. This map corresponds with a gradation of national membership or citizenship in society based on competence. Herrnstein and Murray introduce a five-tiered hierarchy: "the Very Bright," "the Bright," "the Normal," "the Dull," and "the Very Dull":

> The twentieth century dawned on a world segregated into social classes defined in terms of money, power and status. The ancient lines of separation based on hereditary rank were being erased, replaced by a more complicated set of overlapping lines. Social standing still played a major role. . . . Our thesis is that the twentieth century has continued the transformation, so that the twenty-first will open on a world in which cognitive ability is the dividing force. The shift is more subtle than the previous one but more momentous. Social class remains the vehicle of social life, but the intelligence pulls the train. (p. 25)

Following this claim the authors go on to maintain:

> Low intelligence is a stronger precursor of poverty than low socioeconomic background. Whites with IQs in the bottom 5 percent of the distribution of cognitive ability are fifteen times more likely to be poor than those with IQs in the top 5 percent. (p. 127)

The cognitive map charts nature's differential order of endowments to different groups of human beings. It is nobody's fault that there is inequality in the land. Indeed, our best political efforts to wipe out such inequality only compound the bad hand that nature has dealt to "the dull" and "the very dull." This is what liberal politicians did in the '60s. They gave handouts to the poor, the low-IQ types, the congenital criminals and the welfare sororities. The consequences everywhere were bad, but particularly bad for the poor:

The irony is that as America equalizes the circumstances of people's lives, the remaining differences in intelligence are increasingly determined by differences in genes. . . (p. 91)

Ultimately, for Herrnstein and Murray, liberal policies elaborated in the '60s aimed at helping poor Americans overly politicized the function of government in people's lives. The best thing that the government can now do is to step aside and let the law of nature and the invisible hand of the market re-establish a necessary equilibrium in social life. For these authors, the removal of impediments to the efficient sorting of cognitive capacity is the key to national renewal and national well being.

CONCLUSION

The Bell Curve must be viewed against the backdrop of a deeply conservative phase in the evolution of the American polity. This new phase in American life is reflected in ever more conservative in-roads into the academy itself. A significant correlate of these developments has been the deep incorporation of academic scholarship into the culture industry. This is reflected particularly in the ever-expanding commerce of fast-break quasi-academic books aimed at mass consumption that blur the lines between academic scholarship, policy, and entertainment. To put the matter bluntly, right-wing academics have learned that writing panic prose, writing that manipulates authoritarian popular anxieties and desires, sells well. Herrnstein and Murray's *The Bell Curve* joins a steady stream of doomsday books—such as *The Closing of the American Mind* (1987), *Cultural Literacy* (1987), *The Disuniting of America* (1992), *Illiberal Education* (1991), *Alien Nation* (1995), and Murray's own *Losing Ground* (1984)—that focus attention on the internal threats to national identity and national security. Herrnstein and Murray's discussion of citizenship marks the aggressive resurgence of biological arguments in the discussion of the social policy regarding some of the most intractable political and social problems in contemporary American society.

The lived reality in the United States is that though formally citizens, some groups of Americans, particularly working-class blacks and Latinos, occupy the place of modern-day plebeians; that is to say, they are treated as second class citizens. There is solid social, economic, and cultural evidence that this is so. In *The Bell Curve*, Herrnstein and Murray, with great fanfare, wipe this evidence away, pointing instead to the relative imperfection of the mental structures of America's lower classes. In their hands, biology becomes a powerful tool for the legitimation of unequal status. The very bright and the very dull are two different types of citizens. One type of citizen lives at the top of the food chain in the hallowed suburb, while the other lives at the bottom in the inner city. Herrnstein and Murray contend that there is not much that government should do about this. Indeed, current policies of government handouts and uncontrolled immigration are leading us down the slippery slope of dysgenesis—the precipitous fall in IQ—as the least endowed multiply and procreate without restraint. This perhaps will be the end of America as we know it. And then what? . . . Maybe, the plebeians will inherit the earth.

8

THE DEVIL FINDS WORK
Re-reading Race and Identity in Contemporary Life

As a result of the massive proliferation of reproductions, we have become awash in signs, signs which have become, free floating, detached from any original signified, and thus infinitely self-referential.

—Rupert Berk, "Sightseeing and Virtual Sightseeing," p. 5

We have now reached a state in modern society where this integration must take place or the complexity and antagonisms of society will destroy the personality.

—C.L.R. James, *American Civilization*, p. 151

Oh god, I feel I am falling.

—Madonna, "Like a Prayer"

INTRODUCTION

We are living in new racial times, new racial circumstances. Racial dangers have multiplied, but so have the possibilities for renewal and change. We are living in a historical moment in which the racial order is being reconfigured in the tiniest crevices of everyday life. As I have stressed throughout this book, we need new ways to talk about race and identity to help us better understand the powerful rearticulations that are taking place in popular culture and in the commonsense of the whole body politic. One of these significant new developments is the growing anxiety and restlessness that characterize the white middle class. This tumult and restlessness are most strongly foregrounded at the level of the production of identities and representations. We are living in a time of the production of crass identity politics. By identity politics I mean the strategic deployment of the discourse of group distinctiveness in everyday struggles over political representation and scarce resources (the distribution of goods and services) in education and society. Far too often, identity politics are discussed in ways that suggest that only minority groups—particularly African Americans and Latinos—practice, promote, and benefit from identity politics. The case may further be made that minorities are the only ones who experience the effects of these politics in terms of the fragmentation of identity and symbolic and social disorientation and dislocation. This is manifestly false; white people also practice and benefit from identity politics. Nowhere is this more powerfully registered than in popular culture. As indicated earlier, one has only to look at the respective coverage of whites and minorities on the evening news to see the coordinating role the media play in the elaboration of white identity and the corresponding disorganization and subversion of minority identity formation.

In this chapter, I try to understand these developments in racial identity formation and popular culture. Attention is directed to the twin processes of racial simulation (or the constant fabrication of racial identity through the production of the pure space of racial origins) and resentment (the process of defining one's identity through the negation of the other [Nietzsche, 1967].) I look at the operation of these two processes in popular culture and in education. I argue that these processes operate in tandem in the prosecution of the politics of racial affiliation and racial exclusion in our times.

RECODING RACIAL IDENTITY

In his book, *Simulations*, Jean Baudrillard (1983, p. 1) recounts a story told by the Latin American writer, Jorge Luis Borges. It is the story of some special mapmakers, the Cartographers of the Empire, who draw up a map so detailed that it ends up covering the entire territory that was the object of the Cartographers' mapmaking. Baudrillard uses the fable to announce the ushering in of the epoch of simulation, our age, the age in which the real is replaced by the hyperreal and the line between reality and fiction is forever deferred. The photo opportunity is our only contact with the president. The Patriarch only blooms in Autumn. The copy has in this case completely usurped the original.

There is no place like home anymore in this new world order of boundary transgression and constantly collapsing global space.

I will take up the Borges story as a point of departure in my exploration of the articulation of race relations and racial identities in popular culture and education at the end of the century. In doing so, I draw directly on Baudrillard's ostensible theme in the above passage that recounts the trials and tribulations of the Emperor's Cartographers—the centrality of simulation in our contemporary age. For the idea of the copy that constantly recodes, usurps, and appropriates the original is a very precise insight into the way in which racial difference operates in popular culture and intellectual life. It is this theme of simulation that I will return to, but let me first say that I believe that Borges's allegory is a fable about identity which I understand to be a drama of social crisis and recuperation, of exclusion and affiliation, of exile and return. Racially dominant identities do depend on the constant ideological appropriation of the other. Racial identity, racial affiliation, and racial exclusion are the products of human work, human effort (Said, 1993). The field of race relations in popular culture, but also in education, is a field of simulation. The story of mapmaking is also a story, ultimately, of the excess of language that is involved in racial discourse. There is always something left over in language that never allows us to gather up our racial identities in one place and to fix them in invariant racial slots. The Emperor needs the Empire. The Emperor exists for the fact of Empire. Without it, he does not exist. Worst yet, as Baudrillard might suggest, without the Empire, he does not know himself to exist. He is like the Devil-Landlord in Derek Walcott's *Ti Jean and His Brothers* (1970) who wants to drink at the pool of mortality. He wants to be human. But the peasants will burn down his Great House. The Landlord is a homeless Devil.

As I noted earlier, understanding the operation of racial logics in education, paradoxically, requires an understanding of their constant simulation outside the laboratory of the educational field itself—in literature and popular culture, in the imaginary. It is this blend of the educational and the popular that I want to explore briefly here, for one of the current difficulties in the educational literature on race relations is its refusal of the popular. American middle-class white youth and adults know more about inner-city blacks through the media, particularly, television and film, than through personal or classroom interaction or even in textbooks. Nowadays, textbooks are looking intertextually more and more like TV with their HD graphics and illustrations and their glossy, polysemic treatment of subject matter. In addition, anti-institutional educational projects such as Teach For America[1]—with its mission to save the urban poor for god, for capitalism, and for country—are deeply inscribed in a language of the racial other pulled off the television set, as we will see in a moment. We live in a time when "pseudo-events"—as Daniel Boorstin (1975) called media-driven representations in the '70s—have usurped any relic of reality beyond that which is staged. Media simulations have driven incredibly deep and perhaps permanent wedges of difference between the world of the suburban dweller and his inner-city counterpart. Argues Boorstin (1975, p. 3) "we have used our wealth, our literacy, our technology, and our progress, to create a thicket of unreality which stands between us and the facts of life." It is these "facts of life"—notions of what, for example, black people are like or what Latinos are like—that are invented and reinvented in the media, in popular magazines in the newspaper and in television and popular film. In this sense, popular culture is always a step ahead of educational institutions in terms of strategies of incorporation and mobilization of racial identities. As authors such as Katherine Frith (1997) point out, by the end of the teenage years, the average student will have spent more time watching television than he or she would have spent in school. It is increasingly television and film, more so than the school curriculum, that educate American youth about race.

THE WAR OVER SIGNS

Even more crucially, to take up further the implications of Baudrillard's *Simulations*, contemporary conflicts in education and in popular culture are fundamentally battles over signs and the occupation and territorialization of symbolic as well as material resources and urban and suburban space. Central to these developments is the rise of resentment politics. In his *Genealogy of Morals* (1967), Friedrich Nietzsche conceptualized resentment as the specific practice of identity displacement in which the social actor consolidates his own identity by complete disavowal of the merits and existence of his social other. This practice of ethnocentric consolidation and cultural exceptionalism now characterizes much of the tug-of-war over educational reform and multiculturalism. This battle over culture, self, and group has spread throughout society as a whole. Resentment and racial reaction therefore define school life as expressed by the extent to which the culture war over signs and identity in the practices has infiltrated everyday life. Education is indeed a critical site in which struggles over the organization and concentration of emotional and political investment and moral affiliation are taking place. These battles over identity involve the powerful manipulation of group symbols and strategies of articulation and rearticulation of public slogans and popular discourses. These signs and symbols are used in the making of identity and the definition of social and political projects.

An important feature of these developments is the radical recoding and re-narration of public life now taking place. As I noted in "Reading the American Popular," traditional distinctions between conservatives and liberals, Democrats and Republicans, the Left versus the Right have collapsed. Radically distorting and conservative energies and drives have taken over the body politic, displacing concerns about inequality and poverty. What we have is the mushrooming of opportunistic discourses activated within the suburban middle class itself. These discourses center on the protection of the home and the defence of the neighborhood from inner-city predators. They narrate the preservation of the nostalgic ancestral record of the group and its insulation from the contaminating racial other. These opportunistic discourses spawned within the last decade and a half foreground new priorities in the public arena: concerns with identity, history, popular memory, nation, family, crime, and so on, now drive the engines of popular will and the public imagination. This shift away from the issue of social inequality of the '60s and '70s means that America is now willing to spend more on law enforcement and prisons than it is on educating inner-city youth. On the other hand, some minority advocates seem more preoccupied with cultural assertion and cultural distinctiveness than with the bruising socio-economic isolation of minority youth.

I look briefly at the mise-en-scène of these cultural discourses associated with the tug-of-war of racial strife in the educational and social life of a divided society—the United States. I particularly highlight for analysis four discourses of racial difference now in use inside and outside of education in which metaphors and symbols of identity and representation are the "issues at stake." These discourses are the following.

First, there is the *discourse of racial origins* (as revealed, for example, in the Eurocentric/Afrocentric debate over curriculum reform). Discourses of racial origins rely on the simulation of a pastoral sense of the past in which Europe and Africa are available to American racial combatants without their modern tensions, contradictions, and conflicts. For Eurocentric combatants such as William Bennett (1994) or George Will (1989), Europe and America are a self-evident and transcendent cultural unity. For the Afrocentric combatants, Africa and the diaspora are one "solid identity," to use the language of Molefi Asante (1993). Proponents of Eurocentrism and Afrocentrism are themselves proxies for larger impulses and desires for stability among the middle classes in American society in a time of constantly changing demographic and economic realities. The immigrants are coming. Jobs are slipping overseas into the third world. Discourses of Eurocentrism and Afrocentrism travel in a time warp to an age when the gods stalked the earth. These discourses of racial origins provide imaginary solutions to groups and individuals who refuse the radical hybridity that is the historically evolved reality of the United States and other major Western metropolitan societies.

The second example of the discourses of resentment is the *discourse of nation*. This discourse is foregrounded in a spate of recent ads by multinational corporate concerns such IBM, United, American Airlines, MCI, and General Electric (GE). These ads both feed on and provide fictive solutions to the racial anxieties of the age. They effectively appropriate multicultural symbols and redeploy them in a broad project of coordination and consolidation of corporate citizenship and consumer affiliation. The marriage of art and economy, as Stuart Ewen (1988) defines advertising in his *All Consuming Images*, commingles with the exigencies of ethnic identity and nation. These multicultural ads directly exploit difference—different races, different landscapes, different traditions and symbols. One moment the semiotic subject of advertising is a free American citizen abroad in the open seas, sailing up and down the Atlantic or the translucent aquamarine waters of the Caribbean sea, or lounging on the pearly white sands of Bermuda or Barbados. In another moment, the free American citizen is transported to the pastoral life of the unspoiled, undulating landscape of medieval Europe. Yet another vista reveals our American Nostromo at one with the beautiful wild life of the forests of Africa—African forests that are just part of the scenery of one of our prominent entertainment parks.

GE's "We Bring Good Things to Life" ad is a very good example of this kind of racial recoding. In this ad, which is shown quite regularly on CNN and ABC, GE is represented as the benevolent corporate citizen extending American technology to Japan, bringing electricity to one Japanese town. Echoes of America's domination and vanquishing of Japan during the Second World War fill the atmosphere of this ad, thereby, glibly eliding contemporary American anxieties about Japan's technological capabilities and possible economic superiority. Corporate advertising conducts its pedagogy via television, providing the balm for a troubled people in pursuit of origins. Ethnicity and race constitute some of the new productive locations for marketing—the new home ports for multinational corporations in search of harbor in the rough seas of international commerce.

Third, there is the *discourse of popular memory and popular history*. This discourse suffuses the nostalgia films of the last half decade. Films such as *Dances with Wolves* (1990), *Bonfire of the Vanities* (1990), *Grand Canyon* (1993), *Falling Down* (1993), *Disclosure* (1995), *Time to Kill* (1996), and *Forrest Gump* (1994) foreground a white middle-class protagonist who appropriates the subject position of racial "victim." For example, Joel Schumaker's *A Time to Kill* offers pedagogical insight about social problems concerning difference from the perspective of the embattled white suburban dweller. The problem with difference is, in Schumaker's world, symptomatic of a crisis of feeling for white suburban middle classes—a crisis represented in blocked opportunity and wished fulfillment, overcrowding, loss of jobs, general insecurity, crime, and so forth. The contemporary world has spun out of order, and violence and resentment are the coping strategies of white middle-class actors.

In *A Time to Kill*, Schumaker presents us with the world of the "New South," Canton, Mississippi, in which social divides are extreme and blacks and whites live such different lives they might as well have been on separate planets. This backwater of the South serves as a social laboratory to explore a burning concern of suburban America: retributive justice. When individuals break the law and commit acts of violent anti-social behavior then the upstanding folks in civil society are justified in seeking their expulsion or elimination. The film poses a rather provocative question: When, in short, is it respectable society's "Time to Kill." Are there circumstances in which retribution and revenge and resentment are warranted? The makers of *A Time to Kill* say resoundingly "Yes." This answer is impervious to class or race or gender.

In order to make the case for retributive justice, Schumaker puts a black man at the epicenter of this white normative discourse—what Charles Murray (1984) calls "white popular wisdom." What would you do if your ten-year-old daughter is brutally raped and battered, pissed on, and left for dead? You would want revenge? This is a role-play that has been naturalized in society to mean white victim, black assailant— the Willy Horton shuffle. In *A Time to Kill*, the discourse is inverted: The righteously angry are a black worker and his family. Two redneck assailants raped his daughter. Carl Lee, the black lumberyard worker, gets even with the two callous criminals by shooting them down on the day of their arraignment. One brutal act is answered by another. One is a crime, the other is righteous justice. Crime will not pay. In this revenge drama, the message of retributive justice is intended to override race and class lines. We are living in a time when "an eye for an eye" prevails. The racial enemy is in our private garden. In the face of bureaucratic incompetence we have to take the law into our own hands.

These films also retell national history from the perspective of bourgeois anxieties. Hence, in *Forrest Gump*, the peripatetic Gump interposes himself into the raging decade of the '60s, stealing the spotlight from the civil-rights movement, Vietnam War protestors, the feminist movement, and so forth. Public history is overwhelmed by personal consumerism and wish fulfillment. "Life is," after all, "just a box of chocolates. You never know what you might get." You might get Newt Gingrich. But who cares. History will absolve the American consumer.

The fourth example of resentment is the discourse of bourgeois *social voluntarism*. This is an example of what I wish to call positive resentment—a resentment based on what can best be described as a post-Reaganite selfish idealism. One of the most powerful examples of this discourse is provided in Teach For America's (TFA) highly ideologically motivated intervention in the education of the inner-city child. This is a voluntarism that is backed by the leading corporations in the country such as Xerox, IBM, Ross Perot, and Union Carbide. TFA's scarcely veiled agenda is to undermine and discredit teacher education preparation in the university and the teacher certification process as it presently exists. For TFA, the inner-city child is the tragic ballast weighing down the ship of state. By helping the inner-city child, the good TFA recruit can be projected as a timely hero rescuing society from inner-city degeneracy: crack, crime, and procreation. This is all powerfully represented in TFA's recruitment brochures and promotional literature. Of course, crime prevention tops the list of these green beret recruits, and crime and violence is presented in one recruitment manual as naturally residing in the heart of the inner-city child. The TFA recruit must prepare himself for the pseudonormative task of crime prevention:

> Let's . . . pretend that I'm one of your students, named [use your name] and we're going to act out a scene. So, don't tell me what you would do, just do it. Don't tell me what you would say, just say it. I'm going to take out a knife [your pen] in a non-threatening manner. School rules prohibit knives in the building, but some teachers look the other way. Begin. (Teach For America, 1990, p. 22)

It is striking how TFA's representation of the inner-city child seems to be skimmed directly from the surface of the television set. The world of the inner city is available to the middle-class actor through simulation.

CONCLUSION

Against the grain of historical variability, a present irony exists with respect to racial identity formation. That is, whereas educators insist on the master narratives of homogeneity and Western culture in their headlong retreat from diversity and hybridity, the captains and producers of the culture industry readily exploit the ambiguities of racial identity formation. Even cultural nationalism and Afrocentrism can sell goods and services. A good example is the hot trading and hawking of the image of Malcolm X that took place in the early nineties—the assortment of items, from the "X" cap to the glossy cover designs of magazines such as *Newsweek*, the *New Yorker* and the *New York Times Sunday Magazine* that have placed a bill of sale on the great icon. Needless to say, Eurocentrism has also been incorporated in advertising as in the United ad that pitches a trip to a homogeneous imperial England free of the presence of the immigrant populations that have entered the Mother Country from every corner of England's once vast commonwealth.

It is precisely this rearticulation and recoding that I call nonsynchrony. Racial difference and identities, as Edward Said (1993) points out, are produced. I therefore want to call attention to the organization and arrangement of racial relations of domination and subordination in cultural forms and ideological practices in the mass media and in education—what Louis Althusser calls the "the mise-en-scène of interpellation." I am interested in the way in which moral leadership and social power are exercised in the "concrete" in this society and globally. In the past, I have pointed to the impact of these discontinuities among differently situated groups of minorities. Here, I have tried to draw attention to these dynamics as they operate in debates over identity and curriculum reform, hegemonic cultural assertions in advertising, popular film, and in the educational voluntarism of the much publicized project called Teach For America, "Our Peace Corps at home."

What do these examples of racial simulation and resentment tell us about the contemporary state of race relations in education and society? Collectively, they point to a generalized pattern of revision and recoding of our racial landscape. They also point to an instability in the elaboration of national racial categories and identities in late-twentieth-century society. In part, these examples invoke the new depthlessness, radical eclecticism, and rampant nostalgia of the age. In the shadow between truth and fiction lies the new reality of racial formation in our contemporary era. On the one hand, this is an age in which the emergence of subaltern racial minorities, their demands for democratic participation and the assertion of their heritages and identities have precipitated a sense of moral panic and a series of quixotic and contradictory responses within the educational establishment that link conservative intellectuals and born again liberals in the academy to some of the more vulgar anti-intellectual and fundamentalist political groups and traditions in this country. This is summarized in the politics of clarity and the chants of political correctness and reverse discrimination that now provide the ideological cover for that special species of low flying behaviorism that has been unloaded by right in all spheres of American cultural life. On the other hand, these new ethnicities are being rapidly colonized, incorporated, and reworked by a culture industry that radically appropriates the new to consolidate the past. Diversity can sell visits to theme parks as well as it can sell textbooks. Diversity can sell AT&T long distance calling cards as well as the new ethnic stalls in the ethereal hearths of the shopping mall, and sometimes, in the most earnest of ways, diversity lights up the whole world and makes it available to capitalism.

Unlike Borges' map, this does not exhaust the subaltern imagination and the transformative character of new epiphanies. This period of multinational capital is witness to the ushering in of the multicultural age—an age in which the empire has struck back, and first world exploitation of the third world has so depressed these areas of the world that there has been a steady stream of immigrants from the periphery seeking better futures in the metropolitan centers. With the rapid growth of the indigenous minority population in the United States, there is now a formidable cultural presence of diversity in every sphere of cultural life. If this is an era of the post, it is also an era of the multicultural, and the challenge of this multicultural era is the challenge of living in a world of difference. It requires generating a mythology of social interaction that goes beyond the model of resentment which seems so securely in place in these times. It means that we must take seriously the implications of the best intuition in the Nietzschean critique of resentment as the process of identity formation that thrives on the negation of the other. The challenge is to embrace the other—to think of a politics that calls on the moral resources of all who are opposed to the power block. The multicultural era therefore poses new, though "difficult," tactical and strategic challenges to subaltern intellectuals and activists. A strategy that seeks to address these new challenges must involve as a first condition the recognition that our differences of race, gender, and nation are merely the starting points for new solidarities and new alliances, not the terminal stations for depositing our agency and identities or the extinguishing of hope and possibility. . . .

NOTE

1.   For more details on Teach for America see chapter 5, "Reading the American Popular."

9

THE USES OF CULTURE

(with Nadine Dolby and Angharad Valdivia)

Caliban: *This island's mine, by Sycorax my mother*
Which thou tak'st from me. When thou cam'st first
Thou strok'st me, and made much of me; wouldst give me
Water with berries in't and teach me how
To name the bigger light, and how the less,
That burn by day and night: and then I lov'd thee,
And show'd thee all the qualities o' th' isle,
The fresh springs, brine-pits, barren place and fertile:
Curse be that I did so!

— William Shakespeare, *The Tempest*

I came by another way, river by river, street after street,
city by city, one bed and another,
forcing the salt of my mask through a wilderness;
and there, in the shame of the ultimate hovels,
lampless and fireless, lacking bread or a stone or a stillness,
alone in myself, I whirled at my will,
dying the death that was mine.

— Pablo Neruda quoted in June Jordan's *Passion*, p. xvi

If the ideas originated in the West Indies it was only in England and in
English life and history that I was able to track them down and test them.
To establish his own identity, Caliban, after three centuries, must himself,
pioneer into regions Caesar never knew.

— C.L.R. James, *Beyond a Boundary*, p. xix

INTRODUCTION

This chapter seeks to promote a rethinking of constructs such as culture, identity, and the relations between centers and peripheries. With Nadine Dolby and Angharad Valdivia, I want to argue that these concepts and relations are far more dynamic than the ways in which they are normally conceptualized in educational research. The dynamism and heterogeneity of everyday life of the myriad human encounters that produce and reproduce cultures and identities are thwarted in education because even the most radical research continues to be overburdened and weighed down by the legacy of behavioral social science and behavioral psychology. Using this history to guide current research and scholarship, educational theorists and practitioners avoid the complexity of human experience in the negotiation of identity and difference in the classroom.

The tendency to treat the topics of culture, identity, and community simplistically is one of the weaknesses that mars current writing on multiculturalism. One might also argue this is true of the writing on race and culture of some of the most insistent detractors to the multicultural project—proponents of Western culture and its canonization in schooling. For example, Eurocentric proponents of Western culture such as Harold Bloom (1987) and William Bennett (1994), radically oppose the literature associated with the Western canon to the new literatures of minority and postcolonial writers. Here culture, identity, and community are narrowly read as the final property of particular groups based on ethnic origins: the culture and meaning of style of Europe and its descendants in the United States versus the culture and style of minority and third world actors now making demands to diversify the school curriculum. Similarly, proponents of multiculturalism and minority ethnicity-based education also treat culture, identity, and community through a narrow ethnic lens. It is suggested by these proponents of "curriculum for diversity" that since the dominant curriculum thrives on the marginalization of the culture of minorities, that minority identities can only be fully redeemed by replacing the Western and Eurocentric bias of the curriculum with non-Western literature. These ethnicity-based education advocates insist on a Robin Hood approach to curriculum reform: "Robbing Peter to pay Paul." In this opposition of the West to the non-West the gulf is fixed. The die is cast.

In this chapter, we critique the gratuitous opposition of Western canonical literature and traditions to the postcolonial culture and literary traditions of the third world and indigenous minority communities that is now such a prominent feature of debates over multiculturalism and Western culture in education. We argue that this opposition is illegitimate, and furthermore, it is not empirically based. As Edward Said (1993) points out, even a cursory glance at the literature of Latino, African, African American, Asian, and Caribbean writers reveals a picture that diverges sharply from a popular wisdom that suggests that there is little or no dialogue or interrelationship between the intellectual and aesthetic traditions of the West and the third world. There is, instead, in the writing of both male and female postcolonial writers, a buoyant play of ideas and a vigorous dialogue over themes of authority, privilege, freedom, and culture that override the binary opposition of "the West versus the third world." Within the radical cultural hybridity that is foregrounded in postcolonial and minority literatures, there is a space for the exploration of difference, not simply as a problem, but as an opportunity for a conversation over curriculum reform and the radically diverse communities we now serve in the university and in schools.

By cultural hybridity, we are not talking about some happy process of integration of differences. Instead, we are referring to what Homi Bhabha calls the "return of the gaze of the discriminated back on the eye of power" (Bhabha, 1994, p. 112). We are talking about the interactive, developmental, bricolage of postcolonial knowledge production that produces discontinuity and disquiet for the colonizer. This development is a central force in peripheries and metropolises alike; and postcolonial literature, particularly postcolonial fiction, offers the most vocal announcement of the new multicultural age coming into itself. This hybridization asserts itself in a radical excess of desires and interests, and chooses as its preferred strategies of resistance humor, satire, and parody. More importantly, it chooses to engage with the canonical tradition as if it were its own—reworking, reordering historical ruins with the dispassion of what Walter Benjamin (1977) calls, in his *The Origin of German Tragic Drama*, "melancholy." Melancholy is to be understood here not as sadness and despondency but as a liberating skepticism toward cultural hierarchies and historical ruins. Emergent discourses of multicultural education could profit from a closer look at the complex ways in which literature treats issues of culture, identity, and knowledge production.

This chapter aims to provide a long overdue intervention in the raging debate over postcolonial and minority literatures, canon formation, and multicultural curriculum reform. It is a caution against the tendency toward cultural exceptionalism and cultural purity that informs current Eurocentric and ethnicity-based curriculum reform platforms now rampant in education. Instead, we call attention to the radical cultural hybridity that is the historically evolved reality of human encounters in the modern world, and the implications of this hybridity for curriculum reform. Finally, this essay is part of a larger project to bring a cultural studies perspective to bear on the theory and practice of multiculturalism. As such, it foregrounds historical variability, shifting social contexts and environments, and the inevitable trestles of association between majority and minority literature and cultural form, the canon and the quotidian, and the empire and the postcolony.

POSTCOLONIAL LITERATURE

In a 1984 interview the Cuban novelist and music historian, Alejo Carpentier, spoke extensively about the fact that the Latin American novel of magical realism draws on baroque, poetic and culturally-hybrid impulses that continue to emanate from a cultural stream constantly replenished by the folkways of the Latin American people themselves. To illustrate this point about cultural hybridity, Carpentier tells the story of an intriguing encounter he had while visiting the remote forest community of Turiamo, on the Caribbean coast of Venezuela. Here, the villagers introduced Carpentier to "the Poet"— an illiterate Afro-Latin griot, who was regarded as the keeper of communal history, the people's poet. In this illiterate, itinerant peasant, Carpentier came face-to-face with the multiaccented, polyphonic voice of these anthropologically defined "natives." At a late-night communal gathering, which Carpentier attended, this Afro-Latin griot, "the Poet," recited for his fellow forest dwellers gathered by the sea, extensive passages of eighth-century French Epic verse in the indigenous Aztec language of Nahuatl. Carpentier tells the story this way:

> Let me tell you an anecdote which illustrates the poetic tradition in Latin America. More than twenty years ago, when I was living in Venezuela, my wife and I went to stay in a small fishing village on the Caribbean

coast called Turiamo. There were no hotels, no bars, and you got there by crossing kilometres and kilometres of virgin forest. All the inhabitants of the village were black, there were no schools and almost everyone was illiterate. We soon got to know the village people and they told us about the Poet, a person who enjoyed a great deal of prestige there. He hadn't been to the village for about two months and the people missed him. One day he reappeared, bringing news from other areas. He was a colossal African, illiterate and poorly dressed. I told him I'd like to hear his poetry. "Yes," he replied, "Tonight, by the sea." And that night all the village people, children, old folk, every one, gathered on the beach to wait for the Poet. He took off his hat with a ritual gesture and, looking out to sea, with his deep, somewhat monotonous voice, began in quite acceptable octosyllables to recite the wonderful story of Charlemagne in a version similar to that of the Song of Roland.

That day I understood perhaps for the first time that in our America, wrongly named Latin, where an illiterate black descendant of Yorubas could recreate the Song of Roland—in a language richer than Spanish, full of distinctive inflections, accents, expressions and syntax—where wonderful Nahuatl poetry existed long before Christopher Columbus was born, even before Alfonso the Wise and San Isidoro's *Etymologies*, in our America, there were a culture and a theatrical disposition which gave poetry an importance long lost in many countries in Europe. (Carpentier, 1985, p. 160)

In a similar manner the St. Lucian Poet, Derek Walcott (1993), in his 1992 Nobel lecture, "The Antilles: Fragments of Epic Memory," talks about taking some American friends to a peasant performance of the ancient Hindu epic of Ramayana in a forgotten corner of the Caroni Plain in Trinidad. The name of this tiny village is the happily agreeable, but Anglo-Saxon, "Felicity." The actors carrying out this ritual reenactment are the plain as day East Indian villagers spinning this immortal web of memory, of ancientness and modernity. Here, again, Walcott like Carpentier, is "surprised by sin" at the simple native world unfurling in its utter flamboyance:

Felicity is a village in Trinidad on the edge of the Caroni Plain, the wide central plain that still grows sugar and to which indentured cane cutters were brought after emancipation, so the small population of Felicity is

East Indian, and on the afternoon that I visited it with friends from America, all the faces along its road were Indian, which as I hope to show was a moving, beautiful thing, because this Saturday afternoon Ramleela, the epic dramatization of the Hindu epic of Ramayana, was going to be performed, and the costumed actors from the village were assembling on a field strung with different-colored flags, like a new gas station, and beautiful Indian Boys in red and black were aiming arrows haphazardly into the afternoon light. Low blue mountains on the horizon, bright grass, clouds that would gather colour before the light went. Felicity! What a gentle anglo-Saxon name for an epical memory. (Walcott, 1993, p. 1).

Carpentier and Walcott's vivid vignettes point toward the complex flow of humanity across presumptive borders. What these authors highlight is the radical encounter of ancient and modern peoples in postcolonial cultures, and the unanticipated trestles of affiliation that link up disparate populations. These writerly stories highlight the difficulty, indeed the futility, of atavistic attempts to maintain group purity, neonationalist-inspired attempts to separate cultural traditions as the basis of some new cultural or social regime.

But the founding of postcolonial literature is not simply to be located in the periphery; it most certainly must be located in the metropole as well. The complex humanity of an already culturally ruined, half-made third world people has spread its tentacles into the first. The postcolonial novel is ultimately a creation of forces of cultural modernization: huge dually destabilizing and integrative logics at home and abroad. The postnational travellers of Mexico, Nigeria, or Bombay greet London or Paris or Toronto or New York City with loudly announced intentions to hang around for awhile.

Latin American and postcolonial literature, in the words of Octavio Paz (1990), have often been "a reply" to European traditions. Postcolonial literature exists in a critical dialogue with first world literature. In this sense, George Lamming's *The Pleasures of Exile* (1984) is a direct response to William Shakespeare's *The Tempest*. Here, Lamming calls attention to issues of language and identity and the master-slave relationship. For Lamming, Caliban's ensnarement by Prospero's gift of language reveals the mask that covers the face of it. Language is not a system of nomenclature in which words innocently name things already out there in the world. Rather, language is deeply wrapped up in the reproduction of social power, the coordination of hierarchies of identity, and the project of colonial subordination and its neocolonial variations. In the seductions and impositions of Prospero's language, Caliban is constrained to see the world through Prospero's motivated categories. But this encounter between Caliban and Prospero allows for Caliban's rearticulation and reinvention of imposed tradition—Caliban has the capacity to curse.

Similarly, Chinua Achebe's *Things Fall Apart* (1969) is a reply to Joseph Conrad's *Heart of Darkness*. In this novel (the title of which is borrowed from W. B. Yeats's poem, "The Second Coming"), Achebe responds to the moment of aporia in Conrad's construction of Africa as featureless, as a vast expanse of blankness. Achebe's fiction provides an historical account of colonial expansion in Nigeria and its destructive, corrosive effects on the Yoruba people and culture. At another level, Achebe's central character Okonwo is like a Michael Henchard in Thomas Hardy's *The Mayor of Casterbridge* (1994) caught between tradition and change, unable to grasp the future. In a similar manner, Toni Morrison's Jadine in *Tar Baby* (1981) is a liminal character caught between two worlds: one white, one black. When she visits the down-home Southern black community, Eloe, with her lover, Son, she is unable to connect with the stifling traditional values and folkways of the people of Son's origins. The loud *kaboom* which she hears when she is left alone in the Eloe community indicates her alienation from the place. Morrison's here alludes to the echo that Adela Quested hears in the Malabar Caves in E. M. Forster's *A Passage to India* (1984).

In *The Dragon Can't Dance* (1979), a novel written by the Trinidadian writer, Earl Lovelace, one of the characters, a lunatic called Taffy, announces his own fake-crucifixion as a modern day christ. He is the self-appointed messiah, an unrecognized martyr willing to die a classical death by stoning. But when he feels the first impressions of real stones pelted by his jeering friends, he hastily abandons his project and literally hurries down from the cross:

> This is the hill tall above the city where Taffy, a man who say he is
> Christ, put himself up on a cross one burning midday and say to his fol
> lowers: "Crucify me! Let me die for my people. Stone me with stones as
> you stone Jesus, I will love you still." And when they start to stone him

in truth he get vex and start to cuss: "Get me down! Get me down," he
say. Let every sinnerman bear his own blasted burden; who is I to die for
people who ain't have sense enough to know that they can't pelt a man
with big stones when so much little pebbles lying on the ground."
(Lovelace, 1979, p. 31)

The mock-religious chiding here is all good fun. But like Jamaica Kincaid, in her travel book, *A Small Place* (1988) and V. S. Naipaul in *Mimic
Men* (1969), Lovelace intends to launch an attack on the idea of the
necessary centrality of the hero-figure in Western literature, and his real
life postcolonial counterpart, the self-deluded, pretentious politician
who almost never delivers on his promises.

Finally, Latin American women writers such as Isabel Allende and
Julia Alvarez reply to more than a particular Western book or hero-
centered narrative. Indeed they intervene in the process of history by
fictionally filling in the gaps of the official record. In *How the García
Girls Lost Their Accent* (1991), Alvarez details some of the social
processes leading up to the U.S. supported coup of 1964 in the
Dominican Republic. Similarly, in both *La Casa de los Espíritus* (1982)
and *De Amor y Sombra* (1984), Allende provides a rich, sweeping picture
of Chilean politics, history, and culture. Both of the authors depict this
picture by de-centering the hero by having a number of speakers,
mostly female, problematize the political nature of quotidian life
throughout the narrative. Yolanda in *How the García Girls Lost Their
Accent* (1991) and Clara in *La Casa de los Espíritus* (1982) surface and dis-
appear to underscore the persistence of women in the historical process
even when they are manifestly absent.

IMPLICATIONS FOR THE CURRICULUM

The postcolonial proposition that culture is radically hybrid has sharp
implications for the dominant curriculum and the emergent discourses
of multiculturalism that continue to represent culture and identity in
static and a-theoretic terms. In this section, we will discuss three of
those implications: first, that proponents of multicultural education
must cease to understand culture and identity in static and a-theoretic
terms, but instead must highlight the complex interpenetration of
cultures; second, they should do so in a way that brings into view the

subaltern gaze on the eye of power, while simultaneously problematizing the very construct of center and periphery; and finally, proponents must address the contemporary reality of students' lives in a postcolonial, globalized, market-driven world in which schooling is only one of numerous spaces available for the negotiation of both identity and culture.

Towards a Re-Orientation of Culture

Despite the increasing volume and complexity of approaches to multicultural education, there is a continued steadfast avoidance of an engagement with postcolonial and cultural studies oriented scholarship which questions an understanding of culture as reified and essentialist. For example, Erikson's claim (1991, p. B2) that "each minority tradition is a distinct cultural entity" is a common way that multicultural advocates understand and address issues of culture. The United States is metaphorically conceptualized as a mosaic, in which separate and distinct cultural groups contribute to the construction of the whole. Even advocates of multicultural education who are less persuaded by the mosaic metaphor and are more concerned with issues of racism, sexism, equality, and democracy (Grant, 1994; Nieto, 1994) fail to engage with the fact that the terrain on which their theories and practices are built is endlessly shifting and reconfiguring itself, and because of this continuous movement and repositioning, cultures cannot be simply stacked up alongside each other and then separately studied and analyzed. Neither group of multicultural advocates engages with the interpenetration and radical hybridity of cultures, the reality, as Stuart Hall (1992, p. 207) writes, of "our mongrel selves." For example, changing the canon, so that it reflects multiple voices and a diversity of perspectives and experiences, is inadequate because it fails to de-stabilize each cultural group from its steady mooring in a separate port. Gates (1995, p. 7) addresses this issue in his critique of the mosaic metaphor, which, as he writes, is "catchy but unhelpful, if it means that each culture is fixed in place and separated by grout." Instead, Gates prefers to understand relationships between cultures as a conversation. It is in this recognition of an ongoing conversation between cultures which are interwoven and interdependent, and whose very definition depends on the existence and interaction with the other, that there is the possibility of an approach to multiculturalism which foregrounds the complexity of the world. It must be noted that this conversation, as shown by postcolonial writers, is not just carried on by separate individuals but within the very minds and bodies of single postcolonial subjects as they navigate the geo-cultural waters that migration entails (Sandoval, 1991).

Re-Positioning the Gaze

Second, the cultural hybridity which is foregrounded in postcolonial literature moves beyond a simple conceptualization of cultures as mutu-ally generative and informed, but also seeks to view the world through the gaze of the subaltern, which deconstructs the West in the carniva-lesque, the laughter and excess buried in the remains of empire, histor-ical ruins and opulent traditions elaborated in the encounters between Europe and the rest of humanity. For the curriculum, the importance of the gaze of the subaltern lies in the ways in which the West is mobilized and represented. The gaze of power, its norms and assumptions, must be deconstructed. Multicultural education advocates have responded to this challenge through using ethnicity-based affiliations to dismantle "whiteness." Often, next to African-Americans, Latinos, and Native Americans are stacked the identities of Polish-Americans, Italian-Amer-icans, Jewish-Americans, etc. However, this fragmentation of whiteness does nothing to destabilize its construct; instead, there must be a funda-mental understanding of the ways in which whiteness has been mobi-lized and used as a foil for "the other." It is critical to draw attention to the radical instability within Western traditions themselves; this is an instability based not on white ethnic fragmentation, but on an under-standing of political and historical forces which lead to a consolidation of identity. This is particularly true with respect to canon formation. As writers such as Michael Bérubé, Gerald Graff, John Guillory, Dominic LaCapra, Gauri Viswanathan, and Cornel West have pointed out, canon formation is itself a strategy of interpretation of historical crisis— a massive effort to coordinate dominant identities by pasting over breaks and contradictions within hegemonic cultural form. For instance, the canonization of British literature occurred after World War I, in the 1920s and '30s, at a time when Europe was in disarray and the British empire was on the wane (Masterman, 1990). British canon-ization of its literature played a critical role, along with the British Broadcasting Corporation, in cultivating a sense of national identity and a recoding of empire as the "Commonwealth of Nations." While the universities worked toward the canonization of literature, the British Broadcasting Corporation helped to draw the line between high and low-brow cultural form and served to coordinate the standardization of spoken English at home and overseas.

Canonization also prevails in the ways we describe and refer to fiction from the post-colony. Thus we have the emerging genre of *magical realism* to distinguish it from the regular realism which Western fictional writers engage in. The very forms of resistance of humor, satire, and parody are bracketed out and labelled as "aberrant" or dismissed as "other" forms of literature (D'Souza, 1991).

In the classroom, there are several pedagogical practices which flow from foregrounding the deconstruction of the West through critical interrogation of its appearance of stability and ahistoricity. For example, literature must be read contrapuntally: teaching Conrad's *Heart of Darkness* along with Achebe's *Things Fall Apart*, Shakespeare's *Tempest* along with Lamming's *The Pleasures of Exile*. The world must be understood as existing in constant conversation with itself: though the center of the empire attempts to reify itself through representing itself as all that is British or American, this consolidation of power does not go unheard or unchallenged. Instead, it is responded to, deconstructed, and revealed as a patched together, and ultimately fragile, project. An example of this process of deconstructing the West is seen is Jamaica Kincaid's *Lucy* (1990). Lucy, a teenager from the West Indies, travels to New York to become an au pair for Lewis and Mariah's four daughters. Mariah is determined to share with Lucy that which gives meaning and beauty to her life, for example, the daffodils which bloom in spring. Lucy, however, brings a different interpretation to the daffodils:

> But nothing could change the fact that where she saw beautiful flowers I saw sorrow and bitterness. The same thing could cause us to shed tears, but those tears would not taste the same. We walked home in silence. I was glad to have at last seen what a wretched daffodil looked like. (p. 30).

In this passage, Kincaid does not simply lay Lucy's background and culture next to Mariah's. Instead, she forces a confrontation between the two perspectives, one which interrogates Mariah's understanding of daffodils as always representative of beauty and the promise of spring. As Kincaid foregrounds Lucy's gaze, she simultaneously destabilizes

Mariah's feelings toward daffodils. The splendor of daffodils is revealed as a constructed norm: Lucy and Mariah do not circle around the daffodils looking at them from different perspectives—Mariah's perspective is deliberately dissected, scrutinized, and revealed as the unexamined gaze of power.

While it is imperative that the West be destabilized as a fundamental part of the multicultural project, it is also important to question and foreground the very construction of "the West" and "the rest". As Pieterse (1994, p. 131) argues, "The real frontiers between Europe and non-European worlds have been much more blurred and porous than the rhetoric and imagery of "European civilization" suggest. European culture developed in the context of several forms of osmosis." For example, as Said (1993, p. 15) writes,

> Who in India or Algeria today can confidently separate out the British or French component of the past from present actualities, and who in Britain or France can draw a clear circle around British London or French Paris that would exclude the impact of India and Algeria upon those two imperial cities?

Pieterse, Said, and Hall (1992) recognize that Western culture is not a separate entity that developed in isolation, but is a blending and merging of many cultures. Thus, the other is always already present in notions of the West. Similarly, Morrison (1990) unpacks the dichotomy between American and African-American literature, revealing the Africanist presence and influence in writers classified as part of the American canon. These scholars highlight the blurring of boundaries, further questioning multicultural assumptions of distinct cultures which can be arrayed in separate, defined boxes.

Ultimately, the historical and contemporary processes of globalization highlight the fact that the world rotates on relationships more complex than simply center and periphery. Koreans may be more concerned about Japan's influence on their culture than that of the United States (Appadurai 1990), and West Africans may understand their adoption and adaptation of American culture as a form of subverting and contesting French hegemony (Diawara, 1992). We do not mean to deny that cultural flows are uneven, and do acknowledge that hegemonic forces play a considerable role in the process of globalization; however, it is overly simplistic to see globalization as producing only homogeneity and conformity to the United States and Europe. Instead, to fully understand the quotidian experiences of a postcolonial world, it is necessary to take a broader and less deterministic view: one which views power in a Foucauldian sense, and seeks to identify and highlight the breaks, contradictions, and multiple axes of identity in both the center and periphery. Culture, in this equation, becomes a site of both production and contestation: an arena in which struggles are manifest (Grossberg 1994, p. 8).

Understanding Students' Lives: The Production of Identity

Finally, proponents of multicultural education must understand and respond to the globalized, postcolonial world in which students live and produce, not simply reflect, identities. This global cultural flow, which encompasses the movement of people, money, ideas, technology, and the media (Appardurai, 1990) destabilizes the imagining of bounded communities which are solidified through geographic or racialized borders. Students are not simply stepping into pre-configured and solid identities such as African American, Jamaican, Italian, or Mexican, but are both re-inventing and questioning the very constructs of these imagined national and racial communities. For example, Kathleen Hall (1995) documents how British-Sikh teenagers consciously and strategically act British or Indian depending on the geographic and social space in which they are situated. The movement and identities which are produced by these teenagers cannot be easily classified as "British" or "Sikh," and is more than a simple blending of the two: instead these identities are possibly representative of a third space (Bhabha, 1991) which contests the very idea of originary moments. Dan Yon (1995) charts the similarly hybrid identities produced by students in a Toronto high school. Race, as he discusses it, functions not as solid cultural property, but as a discursive category which allows for the possibility of a student who is "White, White" to be recognized as "Black, Real Black," through signifiers such as music, fashion, and social relations (p. 185). For these students, an approach to the curriculum which represents some content and perspective as "Puerto Rican," "British," "Brazilian," or "Russian," has little relevance as, through their lives, they understand the very instability of these categories. It is also important to note that it is not only students in the metropole or the diaspora who experience the shifting nature of identity, and proceed to negotiate that identity through the arena of popular culture. In South Africa, students who have never traveled outside of the city in which they were born still reject essentialized categories of race and culture. For example, in an English class students contest a teacher's notion of what it means to be Zulu. Though the teacher is intent on affirming students' culture through celebrating what he understands to be Zulu practices and customs, students see their Zuluness as produced in the sphere of popular culture: its definition comes not from traditional practices, but from an affinity for certain music, nightclubs and magazines. These students, like the students portrayed in Hall's (1995) and Yon's (1995) studies, position themselves as active producers and agents of culture who are situated within a global system. Multicultural education must account for this reality, or risk becoming an anachronism which alienates the students whose lives it hopes to affect.

CONCLUSION

Our principal concern in this chapter, as I have emphasized throughout this book, is to argue that issues of culture and identity are decidedly less stable than is usually proposed in educational research. While scholars in education have attempted to fix and separate cultures in order to reform the curriculum, they have neglected both the historical and contemporary heterogeneity of human interactions and lives. In contrast, literature and popular culture both provide arenas in which cultural hybridity is displayed, and even flaunted, through tropes such as parody and melancholy. While the field of multicultural education endlessly plods along its narrow path, it ignores the very processes of globalization and hybridity which form the framework for the world of the next century (Valdivia, 1995). Regardless of its romantic longings for pure, bounded communities, students themselves display an impulse and desire for a different future. Like the cyborgs who inhabit postcolonial literature, their hybridity raises new possibilities of community, conflicted but bound together for better or worse. Multicultural education must theoretically and practically engage with a world in which simplistically "real" categories such as race do not hold, yet still have material effects. The complexities of this world must not be masked, but addressed and confronted, in the multicultural world that rages into the twenty-first century.

REFERENCES

Achebe, C. (1969). *Things Fall Apart*. New York: Fawcett Crest.

Allende, I. (1982). *La Casa de los Espíritus*. Barcelona: Plaza y Janés.

———. (1984). *De Amor y Sombra*. México: Edivisión.

———. (1993). *The House of Spirits*. New York: Bantam Books.

Altbach, P. (1987). *The Knowledge Context*. Albany, New York: State University of New York.

———. and Kelly, G. (1978). *Education and Colonialism*. New York: London.

Althusser, L.(1971). "Ideology and Ideological State Apparatuses." In *Lenin and Philosophy and Other Essays* (pp. 127–86). London: Monthly Review.

Alvarez, J. (1991). *How the García Girls Lost Their Accent*. Chapel Hill: Algonquin Books.

———. (1992). "Customs." In D. Poey and V. Suarez [eds.] *Iguana Dreams: New Latino Fiction*.

Amado, J. (1969). *Dona Flor and Her Two Husbands* (trans. by H. Onis). New York: Knopf.

Anderson, E. (1994, May). "The Code of the Streets." *The Atlantic Monthly*, pp. 80–94.

Anzaldúa, G. (1987). *Borderlands/La Frontera: The New Mestiza*. San Francisco: Spinsters.

Appardurai, A. (1990). "Disjuncture and Difference in the Global Cultural Economy." In *Public Culture* 2 (2), pp. 1–24.

Apple, M. W. (1993). *Official Knowledge: Democratic Education in a Conservative Age*. New York: Routledge.

———. (1996). *Cultural Politics and Education*. New York: Teacher's College Press.

———. and L. Weis. (1983). *Ideology and Practice in Schooling*. Philadelphia: Temple University Press.

Arnold, M. (1988). *Civilization in the United States: First and Last Impressions of America*. Boston: Cupples and Hurd.

Arnold, M. (1971). *Culture and Anarchy*. Indianapolis: Bobbs-Merrill Company.

Asante, M. (1993). *Malcolm X as Cultural Hero and Other Afrocentric Essays*. Trenton, New Jersey: Africa World Press.

Awkward, M. (1989). *Inspiriting Influences: Tradition, Revision and Afro-American Women's Novels*. New York: Columbia.

Bakhtin, M. (1981). *The Dialogic Imagination: Four Essays*. ed. M. Holquist. Austin: University of Texas Press.

Balibar, E. and I. Wallerstein. (1991). *Race, Nation, Class: Ambiguous Identities*. New York: Verso.

Barnett, S. (1972). *The Complete Signet Classic Shakespeare*. New York: Harcourt Brace Jovanich.

Bastian, A., N. Fruchter, M. Gittell, C. Greer, and K. Haskins. (1986). *Choosing Equality*. Philadelphia: Temple University.

Baudrillard, J. (1983). *Simulations*. New York: Semiotext(e).

Beatty, J. (1994, May). "Who Speaks for the Middle Class." *The Atlantic Monthly*, pp. 65–78.

Behdad, A. (1993). "Traveling to Teach: Postcolonial Critics in the American Academy." In C. McCarthy and W. Crichlow (eds.), *Race, Identity and Representation in Education* (pp. 40–49). New York: Routledge.

Belsey, C. (1980). *Critical Practice*. London: Methuen.

Benjamin, W. (1977). *The Origin of German Tragic Drama*. Trans. John Osbourne. London: New Left Books.

Bennett, W. (1984, November 28). "To Reclaim a Legacy: Text of the Report of Humanities in Higher Education." *Chronicle of Higher Education*, November 28, pp. 16–21.

Bennett, W. (1994). *The Book of Virtues*. New York: Simon & Schuster.

Berk, R. (1997). *Sight Seeing and Virtual Sightseeing: Tourism, Schooling, and Connectivity*. Unpublished Manuscript, Department of Educational Policy Studies, University of Illinois.

Bernal, M. (1987). *Black Athena: The Afroasiatic Roots of Classical Civilization. Volume 1: The Fabrication of Ancient Greece 1785–1985*. New Brunswick, NJ: Rutgers University Press.

Berube, M. (1992). *Marginal Forces/Cultural Centers: Tolson, Pynchon, and the Politics of the Canon*. Ithaca: Cornell University Press.

Bhabha, H. (1991). "The Third Space: Interview with Homi Bhabha." In J. Rutherford (ed.) *Identity, Community, Culture, Difference* (pp. 207–237). London: Lawrence Wishart.

———. (1994). *The Location of Culture*. New York: Routledge.

Bloom, A. (1987). *The Closing of the American Mind*. New York: Simon & Schuster.

Boorstin, D. (1975). *The Image: A Guide to Pseudo-Events in America*. New York: Antheneum.

Bowles, S. and H. Gintis. (1976). *Schooling in Capitalist America*. New York: Basic Book.

Brathwaite, E. K. (1984). The *History of the Voice*. London: New Beacon.

Brimelow, P. (1995). *Alien Nation*. New York: Random House.

Buchanan, P. (1992). "We Stand with President Bush." C-Span Transcripts (eds.), *1992 Republican National Convention* (pp. 6–9). Lincolnshire, IL: Tape Writer.

Burawoy, M. (1981). "The Capitalist State in South Africa: Marxist and Sociological Perspectives on Race and Class." In M. Zeitlin (ed.), *Political Power and Social Theory* (Vol. 2, pp. 279–335). Greenwich, CT: JAI Press.

Campbell, R. (1987). "Securing the Middle Ground: Reporter Formulas in *60 Minutes*." In *Critical Studies in Mass Communication*, 4 (4), pp. 325–350.

Carnoy, M. (1974). *Education and Cultural Imperialism*. New York: Longman.

Carpentier, A. (1979). *Los Pasos Perdidos*. Trans. by Harriet de Onis. New York: Avon Books.

———. (1985). "The Latin American Novel." In *New Left Review* 154, pp. 159–91.

Carter, M. (1979). "You Are Involved." *Poems of Resistance* (p. 44). Guyana Printers Limited.

Cesaire, A. (1983). *The Collected Poetry*. Trans. by C. Esleman & A. Smith. Berkeley: University of California Press.

Clark, R. (1986). *Breakfast for the World*. Unpublished interview with C. McCarthy.

Clayton, R. (1971). *Mexico, Central America, and the West Indies*. London: John Day.

Conrad, J. (1992). *Heart of Darkness and Other Tales*. New York: Oxford University Press.

Cortes, C. (1986). "The Education of Language Minority Students: A Contextual Model." In California State Department of Education (ed.) *Beyond Language: Social and Cultural Factors in Schooling Language Minority Students*. Los Angeles: Evaluation, Dissemination and Assessment Center, California State University.

Cortez, J. (1978). *Coagulations: New and Collected Poems*. New York: Thunder Mouth Press.

Courtney, R. (1988). "On Culture and Creative Drama." *Youth Theatre Journal* 3 (1), pp. 3–9.

Cudjoe, S. (1980). *Resistance and Caribbean Literature*. New York: Longman.

———. and Cain, W. (1995). *C.L.R. James: His Intellectual Legacies*. Amherst: University of Massachusetts.

Czitrom, D. (1982). *Media and the American Mind: From Morse to McLuhan*. Chapel Hill: University of North Carolina Press.

D'Souza, D. (1991). *Illiberal Education: The Politics of Race and Sex on Campus*. New York: Free Press.

Dash, J. (1992). *Daughters of the Dust: The Making of an African American Woman's Film*. New York: The New Press.

Davis, M. (1992, June 1). "Urban America Sees Its Future In L.A.: Burning All Illusions." *Nation* 254 (21), pp. 743–746.

De Lauretis, T. (1987). *Technologies of Marginality*. New York: MacMillan.

Diawara, M. (1992). "Afrokitsch." In G. Dent (ed.) *Black Popular Culture* (pp. 285–291). Seattle: Bay Press.

Dunn, T. (1993). "The New Enclosures: Racism in the Normalized Community." In R. Gooding-Williams (ed.), *Reading Rodney King* (pp. 178–195). New York: Routledge.

Dyson, M. (1993). "Leonard Jeffries and the Struggle for the Black Mind." In M. Dyson (ed.), *Reflecting Black: African American Cultural Criticism* (pp. 157–163). Minneapolis: University of Minnesota Press.

———. (1996). *Between God and Gangsta Rap*. New York: Oxford.

Eagleton, T. (1984). *The Function of Criticism*. London: Verso.

Edari, R. (1984). "Racial Minorities and Forms of Ideological Mystification." In M. Berlowitz and R. Edari (eds.) *Racism and the Denial of Human Rights: Beyond Ethnicity* (pp. 7–18). Minneapolis: Marxist Educational Press.

Editors. (1982). "Central America: What U.S. Educators Need to Know." *Interracial Books for Children Bulletin*. 3 (2–3). pp. 1–64.

Education Week. (1986, May 14). "Here They Come Ready or Not: An *Education Week* "Special Report on the Ways in which America's Population in Motion is Changing the Outlook for Schools and Society." *Education Week*, pp. 14–28.

El Saadawi, N. (1985). *God Dies by the Nile* (Trans. S. Hetata). London: Atlantic Highland.

Eliot, T. S. (1964) "The Love Song of J. Alfred Prufrock." *Selected Poems* (pp. 11–16). New York: Harcourt Brace Jovanich.

Ellsworth, E. (1989). "Why Doesn't This Feel Empowering? Working Through the Repressive Myths of Critical Pedagogy." *Harvard Educational Review*, 59 (3), pp. 297–324.

EPICA Task Force. (1982). *Grenada: The Peaceful Revolution*. Washington, D.C.: EPICA Task Force.

Erickson, P. (June 26, 1991). "Rather Than Reject a Common Culture, Multiculturalism Advocates a More Complicated Route by Which to Achieve It." In *The Chronicle of Higher Education* 37 (41), pp. B1–B3.

Ewen, S. (1988). *All Consuming Images*. New York: Basic Books.

Fanon, F. (1965). *The Wretched of the Earth*. New York: Grove Press.

———. (1985). *Damnes de la Terre*. Preface de Jean-Paul Sartre. Paris: Decouverte.

Farley, C. J. (1994, December 19). "Patriot Games." *Time*, pp. 50–51.

Fedarko, K. (1993, August 23). "Holidays in Hell." *Time*, pp. 50–51.

Fiske, J. (1990). *Introduction to Communication Studies*. New York: Routledge.

Flickema, T. Kane, P. (1980). *Insights: Latin America*. Columbus, OH: Merrill.

Forster, E. M. (1984). *A Passage to India*. New York: Harcourt Brace Jovanovich.

Foster, H. (1983). (ed.) *The Anti-Aesthetic*. Seattle: Bay Press.

Foucault, M. (1970). *The Order of Things: An Archeology of the Human Sciences*. New York: Pantheon.

———. (1977). *Discipline and Punish: The Birth of the Prison*. Trans. A. Sheridan. New York: Vintage.

Frank, A. G. (1969). *Capitalism and Underdevelopment in Latin America*. New York: Monthly Review Press.

Fraser, R. (1988). Wilson Harris: *The Palace of the Peacock*. In D. Dabydeen (ed.), *Handbook for Teaching Caribbean Literature* (pp. 8–16). London: Heinemann.

Freire, P. (1970). *Pedagogy of the Oppressed* (M.B. Ramos). New York: Seabury.

Frith, K. (1997). (ed.) *Undressing the Ad: Reading Culture in Advertising*. New York: Peter Lang.

Gamoran, A. and M. Berends. (1986). *The Effects of Stratification in Secondary*

Schools: Synthesis of Survey and Ethnographic Research. Madison: National Center on Effective Secondary, University of Wisconsin-Madison.

Garrett, L. (1994). *The Coming Plague.* New York: Farrar, Strauss and Giroux.

Gates, D. (1993, March 29). "White-Male Paranoia." *Newsweek,* pp. 48–53.

Gates, H. (1992). *Loose Canons: Notes on the Culture Wars.* New York: Oxford University Press.

Gates, H. L. (1995). "Multiculturalism: A Conversation Among Different Voices." In D. Levine, R. Lowe, B. Peterson, and R. Tenorio (eds.) *Rethinking Schools* (pp. 7–9). New York: The New Press.

Gerbner, G. (1970). "Cultural Indicators: The Case of Violence in Television Drama." *Annals of the American Association of Political and Social Science,* 338, pp. 69–81.

Gilkes, M. (1975). *Wilson Harris and the Caribbean Novel.* London: Heinemann.

Gill, D. (1982). *Assessment in a Multicultural Society. School Council Report: Geography.* London: Commission for Racial Equality.

Gilroy, P. (1993). *The Black Atlantic: Modernity and Double Consciousness.* Cambridge, MA: Harvard University Press.

Giroux, H. (1985). Introduction to P. Freire's *The Politics of Education.* Boston: Bergin and Garvey.

———. (1992). *Border Crossings: Cultural Workers and the Politics of Education.* New York: Routledge.

———. (1994). *Disturbing Pleasures.* New York: Routledge.

———. (1996). *White Noise: Racial Politics and the Pedagogy of Whiteness.* Unpublished Manuscript. State College, University of Pennsylvania.

Gobineau, A. (1915) *The Inequality of Human Races.* London: Heinemann.

Gould, S. (1981). *The Mismeasure of Man.* New York: W. W. Norton.

Graff, G. (1987). *Professing Literature: Institutional History.* Chicago: University of Chicago Press.

Gramsci, A. (1971). *Selections From the Prison Notebooks.* New York: International Publishers.

———. (1983). *Selections from Prison Notebooks.* [ed. Q. Hoare and G. Nowell-Smith]. New York: International Publishers.

Grant, C. and C. Sleeter. (1989). *Turning on Learning: Five Approaches for Multicultural Teaching Plans for Race, Class, Gender, and Disability.* Columbus, OH: Merrill Publishing Company.

Grant, C. A. (1994). "Challenging the Myths about Multicultural Education." In *Multicultural Education* 2 (2), pp. 4–9.

Grant, L. (1984) "Black Females' Place in Desegregated Classrooms." *Sociology of Education,* 57, pp. 98–111.

———. (1985). *Uneasy Alliances: Black Males, Teachers, and Peers in Desegregated Classrooms.* Unpublished manuscript, Southern Illinois University.

Greenfield, S. (1968). *English Rustics in Black Skin.* New Haven, CT: College University Press.

Grossberg, L. (1992). *We Got to Get out of This Place*. New York: Routledge.

———. (1994). "Bringing It All Back Home: Pedagogy and Cultural Studies." In H. Giroux and P. McLaren (eds.), *Between Borders: Pedagogy and the Politics of Cultural Studies* (pp. 1–28).

Guillory, J. (1990). "Canon." In F. Lentricchia and T. McLaughlin (eds.), *Critical Terms for Literary Study* (pp. 233–249). Chicago: University of Chicago Press.

Hacker, A. (1995). *Two Nations: Black and White, Separate, Hostile, Unequal*. New York: Ballantine Books

Hall, K. (1995). "There's a Time to Act English and a Time to Act Indian: The Politics of Identity Among British-Sikh Teenagers." In S. Stephens (ed.), *Children and the Politics of Culture* (pp. 243–264). Princeton: Princeton University Press.

Hall, S. (1980). "Race, Articulation and Societies Structured in Dominance." In UNESCO, *Sociological Theories: Race and Colonialism*, pp. 305–345. Paris: UNESCO.

———. (1980). "Cultural Studies and the Centre: Some Problematics and Problems." In, S. Hall, D. Hobson, A. Lowe and P. Willis (eds.) *Culture, Media, Language: Working Papers in Cultural Studies, 1972–79* (pp. 15–48). London: Hutchinson.

———. (1981). "Teaching Race." In A. James & R. Jeffcoate (eds.) *The School in the Multicultural Society* (pp. 58–69). London: Harper & Row.

———. (1989). "Cultural Identity and Cinematic Representation. *Framework* 36, pp. 66–81.

———. (1992). "Cultural Studies and Its Legacies." In L. Grossberg, C. Nelson, P. Treichler (eds.), *Cultural Studies* (pp. 277–294). New York: Routledge.

———. (1992). "Our Mongrel Selves." In *New Statesman and Society* 5 (207), pp. 6–8.

———. (1996). "Gramsci's Relevance for the Study of Race and Ethnicity." In Morley, D. and Chen, K. (eds.) *Stuart Hall*. London: Routledge.

Haraway, D. (1990). "A Manifesto for Cyborgs: Science, Technology, and Socialist Feminism in the 1980s." In Linda Nicholson (ed.), *Feminism/Postmodernism* (pp. 190–233). New York: Routledge.

Harding, V. (1983). *There Is a River*. New York: Vintage.

Hardy, T. (1994). *The Mayor of Casterbridge*. London: Wordsworth Editions Limited.

Harris, M. (1968). *The Rise of Anthropological Theory*. New York: Thomas Crowell.

Harris, W. (1960). *The Palace of the Peacock*. London: Faber.

———. (1962). *The Whole Armour*. London Faber.

———. (1970, June). "History, Fable and Myth. In the Caribbean and the Guianas." *Caribbean Quarterly*. 16 (2), (pp. 1–32).

———. (1975). *Companions of the Day and Night*. London: Faber.

———. (1977). *Da Silva da Silva's Cultivated Wilderness*. London: Faber.

———. (1977). *Genesis of the Clowns*. London: Faber.

———. (1985). "A Note on the Genesis of *The Guyana Quartet*." In W. Harris (ed.), *The Guyana Quartet* (pp. 7–14). London: Faber.

———. (1989). "Literacy and the Imagination." In M. Gilkes (ed.), *The Literate Imagination* (pp. 13–30). London: MacMillan.

Henriques, J. (1984). "Social Psychology and the Politics of Racism." (ed.), *Changing the Subject: Psychology, Social Regulation and Subjectivity*. New York: Methuen.

Herrnstein, R. and C. Murray. (1994). *The Bell Curve*. New York: Free Press.

Hirsch, E. D. (1987). *Cultural Literacy: What Every American Needs to Know*. Boston: Houghton Mifflin.

hooks, b. (1994). *Outlaw Culture: Resisting Representations*. New York: Routledge.

Iyer, P. (1993, February 8). "The Empire Writes Back." *Time* (pp. 68–73).

James, C.L.R. (1963) *The Black Jacobins*. New York: Vintage.

———. (1978). *Mariners, Renegades and Castaways: The Story of Herman Melville and the World We Live In*. Detroit: Bewick.

———. (1983). *Beyond a Boundary*. New York: Pantheon.

———. (1993). *American Civilization*. Cambridge, MA: Blackwell.

Jameson, F. (1984, July-August). "Postmodernism, or, The Cultural Logic of Late Capitalism." *New Left Review* no. 146, pp. 59–82.

———. (1986). "Third-World Literature in the Era of Multinational Capitalism." *Social Text* 15, pp. 65–88.

JanMohamed, A. (1987). "Toward a Theory of Minority Discourse." *Cultural Critique*, 6, pp. 5–11.

———. and D. Lloyd. (1987). "Introduction: Minority Discourse—What Is to Be Done?" *Cultural Critique*, 7, pp. 5–17.

Jensen, A. (1969). "How Much Can We Boost IQ." *Harvard Educational Review*, Reprint Series no. 2, pp. 1–23.

———. (1981). *Straight Talk About Mental Tests*. New York: Free Press.

———. (1984). "Political Ideologies and Educational Research." *Phi Delta Kappan*, 65 (7), p. 460.

Jones, J. (1992). "The Accusatory Space." In G. Dent (ed.). *Black Popular Culture* (pp. 106–111). Seattle: Bay Press.

Jordan, J. (1980). "For the Sake of People's Poetry: Walt Whitman and the Rest of Us." In J. Jordan, *Passion* (pp. ix–xxvi). Boston: Beacon.

———. (1980). *Passion*. Boston: Beacon Press.

———. (1985). *On Call: Political Essays*. Boston: South End Press.

———. (1988). "Nobody Mean More to Me Than You and the Future Life of Willie Jordan." *Harvard Educational Review* 58(2), 363–374.

Jordan, W. (1968). *White Over Black: American Attitudes Toward the Negro, 1550–1812*. Baltimore: Penguin Books, pp. 94–95.

Kellman, A. (1991 Spring). "Isle Man." *Graham House Review*, 14, p. 15.

Kellner, D. (1993). *Media Culture*. New York: Routledge.

Kennedy, L. (1992). "The Body in Question." In G. Dent (ed.), *Black Popular Culture* (pp. 106–111). Seattle: Bay Press.

Kimball, R. (1990). *Tenured Radicals. How Politics Has Corrupted Our Higher Education*. New York: Harper.

Kincaid, J. (1988). *A Small Place*. New York: Plume.

————. (1990). *Lucy*. New York: Farrar, Strauss and Giroux.

King, D., and C. Anderson. (1980). *America: Past and Present*. Boston: Houghton Mifflin.

Kinzer, S. (1981). "Isthmus of Violence." *Boston Globe Magazine*, August 18, p. 4.

Kozol, J. (1992). *Savage Inequalities*. New York: Crown.

Kroll, J. (1991, June 10). "Spiking a Fever." *Newsweek*, pp. 44–47.

Lacan, J. (1977). "The Mirror Stage as Formative of the Function of the Eye." *Ecrits* (pp. 1–7). Trans. A. Sheridan. New York: Norton.

Laclau, E. and C. Mouffe (1985). *Hegemony and Socialist Strategy: Toward a Radical Democratic Politics*. London: Verso.

Ladson-Billings, G. and A. Henry. (1990). "Blurring the Borders: Voices of African Liberatory Pedagogy in the United States and Canada." *Journal of Education* 172 (2), pp. 72–87.

Lamming, G. (1984). *The Pleasures of Exile*. London: Allison and Busby.

Lasch, C. (1991). *The True and Only Heaven: Progress and Its Critics*. New York: Norton.

Lerner, G. (1975). "Placing Women in History: Definitions and Challenges." *Feminist Studies* 3 (1–2), 5–15.

Lieberman, P. (1992, June 18). "Fifty-two Percent of Riot Arrests were Latino, Study Says." *Los Angeles Times*, p. B3.

Lineup Police Products (1992), *The Official Cop Catalog*. San Luis Obispo, California: Lineup Police Products, Inc.

Lovelace, E. (1979). *The Dragon Can't Dance*. London: Longman.

Marable, M. (1985). *Black American Politics*. London: Verso.

Marquez, G. G. (1970). *One Hundred Years of Solitude* (Trans. by G. Rabassa). Harper & Row.

Masterman, L. (1990). *Teaching the Media*. New York: Routledge.

McCarthy, C. (1988). "Reconsidering Liberal and Radical Perspectives on Racial Inequality in Schooling: Making the Case for Nonsynchrony." *Harvard Educational Review* 58 (2), pp. 265–279.

————. (1988). "Reconsidering Liberal and Radical Perspectives on Racial Inequality in Schooling," *Harvard Educational Review* 58 (2), 265–279.

————. (1990) *Race and Curriculum*. London: Falmer Press.

————. (1990). *Being There: A Math Collaborative and the Challenge of Teaching Mathematics in the Urban Classroom* (monograph). Wisconsin Center for Educational Research.

————. (1990). *Race and Curriculum*. London: Falmer Press.

————. (1994). "Multicultural Discourses and Curriculum Reform: A Critical Perspective." *Educational Theory* 44 (1), pp. 81–98.

————. (1995). "The Problem With Origins: Race and the Contrapuntal Nature of the Educational Experience." *The Review of Education/Pedagogy/ Cultural Studies* 17(1), pp. 87–105.

———. and M. Apple. (1988). "Race, Class and Gender in American Educational Research: Towards a Nonsynchronous Parallelist Position." *Perspectives in Education* 4 (2), 67–69.

———. and W. Crichlow. (1993). (eds.). *Race, Identity, and Representation in Education* (pp. 3–10). New York: Routledge.

———. and F. Schrag. (1990). Departmental and Principal Leadership in Promoting Higher Order Thinking." *Journal of Curriculum Studies* 22 (6), pp. 529–543.

Melville, H. (1851). *Moby Dick: Or the White Whale*. New York: Harper.

Mercer, K. (1992). "'1968' Periodizing Postmodern Politics and Identity." In L. Grossberg, C. Nelson and P. Treichler (eds.), *Cultural Studies* (pp. 424–449). New York: Routledge.

Morgan, S. (1993, March). "Costal Disturbances." *Mirabella*, p. 46.

Morrison, T. (1977). *Song of Solomon*. New York: Signet.

———. (1981). *Tar Baby*. New York: Plume.

———. (1987). *Beloved*. New York: Knopf.

———. (1989). "Unspeakable Things Unspoken: The Afro-American Presence in American Literature." *Michigan Quarterly Review* 38 (1), pp. 1–34.

———. (1990). "The Site of Memory." In R. Fergusson, M. Gever, T.T. Minh-ha and C. West. *Out There: Marginalization and Contemporary Cultures*. New York: The Museum of Contemporary Art.

———. (1990). *Playing in the Dark*. New York: Vintage Books.

———. (1992). *Jazz*. New York: Knopf.

Morton, S. G. (1839). *Crania Americana or, A Comparative View of Skulls of Various Aboriginal Nations of North and South America*. Philadelphia: John Pennington.

Murray, C. (1984). *Losing Ground: American Social Policy, 1950–1980*. New York: Basics Books.

Naipaul, V.S. (1969). *The Micmic Men*. London: Penguin.

Nieto, S. (1994). "Affirmation, Solidarity, and Critique: Moving Beyond Tolerance in Multicultural Education." In *Multicultural Education* Vol. 1 (4), pp. 9–12, 35–38.

Nietzsche, F. (1967). *On the Genealogy of Morals*. Trans. W. Kaufman. New York: Vintage.

Nkomo, M. (1984). *Student Culture and Activism in Black South African Universities*. Connecticut: Greenwood Press.

O'Connor, J. (1990, April 29). "On TV, Less Separate, More Equal." *The New York Times* (Arts Leisure Section), p. 1.

Oakes, J. (1992). "Can Tracking Research Inform Practice? Technical, Normative, and Political Considerations." *Educational Researcher* 21 (4), pp. 12–21.

Obiechina, E. (1978). *Culture, Tradition and Society in the West African Novel*. London: Heinemann.

Ogbu, J. (1978). *Minority Education and Caste*. New York: Academic Press.
———. and M. Matute-Bianchi. (1986). "Understanding Sociocultural Factors in Education: Knowledge, Identity, and School Adjustment." In California State Department of Education, ed., *Beyond Language: Social and Cultural Factors in Schooling Language Minority Students*. Los Angeles: Evaluation, Dissemination and Assessment Center, California State University.
Okri, B. (1992). *The Famished Road*. New York: Anchor Books.
Omi, M. and H. Winant. (1993). "On the Theoretical Concept of Race." In MacCannell, D. (ed.), (1989). *The Tourist: A Theory of the Leisure Class*. New York: Schocken.
———. (1986). *Racial Formation in the United States* (First Edition). New York: Routledge.
———. (1994). *Racial Formation in the United States* (Second Edition). New York: Routledge.
Ondaatje, M. (1992). *The English Patient*. New York: Vintage.
Parenti, M. (1992). *Make Believe Media: The Politics of Entertainment*. New York: St. Martin's Press.
———. (1993). *Inventing Reality*. New York: St. Martin's Press.
Paz, O. (1990). *In Search of the Present*. New York: Harcourt Brace Jovanovich.
Phillips, C. (1992). *Cambridge*. New York: Knopf.
Pieterse, J. N. (1994). "Unpacking the West: How European is Europe?" in A. Rattansi and S. Westwood (eds.), *Racism, Modernity and Identity* (pp. 129–149). Cambridge: Polity Press.
Pinar, W., Reynolds, W., Slattery, P., and Taubman (1995). *Understanding Curriculum*. New York: Peter Lang.
Postman, N. (1986). *Amusing Ourselves to Death*. New York: Penguin.
Preston, R. (1994). *The Hot Zone*. New York: Random House.
Purkey, S. and R. Rutter. (1987). "High School Teaching: Teacher Practices and Beliefs in Urban and Suburban Public Schools. *Education Policy* 1 (3), pp. 375–393.
Ravitch, D. (1990). "Diversity and Democracy: Multicultural Education in America." *American Educator* 14 (1), pp. 16–48.
Reed, A. (1992). "The Urban Underclass as Myth and Symbol: The Poverty of Discourse About Poverty." In *Radical America* 24 (1), pp. 21–40.
Rist, R. (1970). "Social Class and Teacher Expectations: The Self-Fulfilling Prophecy in Ghetto Education." *Harvard Educational Review*, no. 40, pp. 411–51.
Ross, J. (1967). *Constraints on Variables in Syntax*. (Unpublished Ph.D. Dissertation, Department of Linguistics: M.I.T.).
Roumain, J. (1978). *Masters of the Dew*. Trans. by Langston Hughes and Mercer Cook. London: Fleinemann.
Rushdie, S. (1981). *Midnight's Children*. London: Penguin.
Said, E. (1985 Autumn). "Orientalism Reconsidered." *Race and Class* 27 (2), pp. 1–15.

————. (1993). "The Politics of Knowledge." In C. McCarthy and W. Crichlow (eds.), *Race, Identity and Representation in Education* (pp. 306–314). New York: Routledge.

————. (1993). *Culture and Imperialism*. New York: Knopf.

Sandoval, C. (1991). "U.S. Third World Feminism: The Theory and Method of Oppositional Consciousness in the Postmodern World." *Genders* 10, pp. 1–24.

Sarup, M. (1986). *The Politics of Multiracial Education*. London: Routledge.

Schlesinger, A. (1992). *The Disuniting of America*. New York: Norton.

Schwartz, M. and J. Connor. (1986). *Exploring American History*. New York: Globe.

Senghor, L. (1981). *Poems of Black Orpheus*. Trans. by W. Oxley. London: Menard Press.

Shange, N. (1983). *A Daughter's Geography*. New York: St. Martin's Press.

Smolowe, J. (1993, August 23). "Danger in the Safety Zone." *Time*, pp. 29–32.

Solomon, R. (1990). "Nietzsche, Postmodernism, and Resentment: A Genealogical Hypothesis." In C. Koelb (ed.) *Nietzsche as Postmodernist: Essays Pro and Con* (pp. 267–294). New York: SUNY.

Spring, J. (1991). *American Education: An Introduction to Social and Political Aspects*. Boston: Beacon Press.

Swartz, E. (1990). *Cultural Diversity and the School Curriculum: Context and Practice*. Paper presented at the Annual Meeting of the American Educational Research Association, Boston.

The Syracuse Constitution (1993, August 2). "A Menace to Society." In *The Syracuse Constitution*, p. 5.

Taussig, T. (1980). *The Devil and Commodity Fetishism in South America*. Chapel Hill: University of North Carolina Press.

The Teachers' Committee on Central America. (1982). *El Salvador, the Roots of the Conflict. A Curriculum Guide*. Oakland, CA: The Teachers' Committee on Central America.

Teach For America (1990). *Teach for America Recruitment Manual*. New York: Teach for America.

Thomas, E. (1987). "Lionhearted Women: Sistren Theatre Collective." *Race and Class*. 28 (3), pp. 66–72.

Troyna, B. and R. Hatcher. (1992). *Racism in Children's Lives*. New York: Routlege.

Valdivia, A. N. (1995). *Feminism, Multiculturalism, and the Media: Global Diversities*. London: Sage.

————. (1995) (ed.), "Feminist Media Studies in the Global Setting: Beyond Binary Contradiction and into Multicultural Spectrums." In A. Valdivia (ed.), *Feminism, Multiculturalism and the Media: Global Diversities* (pp. 7–29).

Viadero, D. (1989, May 24). "Schools Witness a Troubling Revival of Bigotry." *Education Week*, p. 1.

Walcott, D. (1970). "Ti Jean and His Brothers." In D. Walcott, *Dream on Monkey Mountain and Other Plays*. (81–166). New York: Farrar, Strauss and Giroux.

———. (1986). *A Far Cry from Africa. Collected Poems: 1948–1984.* (p. 18). New York: Noonday.

———. (1993). *The Antilles: Fragments of Epic Memory.* New York: Farrar, Strauss and Giroux.

Wallace, M. (1990). *Invisibility Blues: From Pop to Theory.* London: Verso.

———. (1992). "*Boyz 'N the Hood* and *Jungle Fever.*" In G. Dent (ed.), *Black Popular Culture* (pp. 123–131). Seattle: Bay Press.

Wallerstein, I. (1991). "Class Conflict in the World Economy." In I. Wallerstein and E. Balibar (eds.). *Race, Nation, Class: Ambiguous Identities* (pp. 115–124). New York: Verso.

Wellman, D. (1977). *Portraits of White Racism.* Cambridge: Cambridge University Press.

West, C. (1993). *Race Matters.* Boston: Beacon Press.

Wexler, P. (1976). *The Sociology of Education: Beyond Equality.* Indianapolis: Bobbs-Merrill.

———. (1992). *Becoming Somebody: Toward the Social Psychology of School.* London: Falmer Press.

Whitty, G. (1985). *Sociology and School Knowledge.* London: Methuen

Will, G. (1989). "Eurocentricity and the School Curriculum. *Baton Rouge Morning Advocate.* December 18, p. 3.

Williams, E. (1964). *Capitalism and Slavery.* London: Andre Deutsch.

Williams, R. (1958). *Culture and Society.* London: Chatto and Windus.

———. (1961). *The Long Revolution.* London: Penguin.

———. (1974). *Television, Technology and Cultural Form.* New York: Schocken Books

Wood, G. (1985). "Schooling in a Democracy: Transformation or Reproduction?" In F. Rizvi (ed.), *Multiculturalism as an Educational Policy* (91–111). Geelong, Victoria: Deakin University Press.

Wood, J. (1993, August). "John Singleton and *The* Impossible Greenback of the Assimilated Black Artist." *Esquire,* pp. 59–108.

Wright, E. (1978). *Class, Crisis and the State.* London: New Left Review.

Yon, D. (1995). *Unstable Terrain: Explorations in Identity, Race and Culture in a Toronto High School.* York University: unpublished Ph.D. dissertation.

INDEX